I'm in the Kitchen, Now What?!™

by Pamela Richards

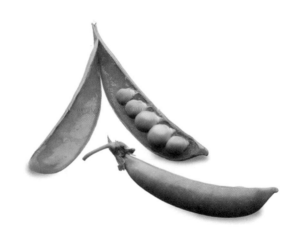

SILVER
LINING
BOOKS

NEW YORK

Copyright © 2000 by Silver Lining Books
ISBN 0760720657

For information contact:
Silver Lining Books
122 Fifth Avenue
New York, NY 10011

First Edition
This edition was published by Silver Lining Books.

Printed and Bound in the United States of America

introduction

KELLY MILLER WAS NERVOUS. FOUR GUESTS WERE DUE TO arrive for dinner in an hour. Could she possibly pull it off? Serve a great dinner, that is. "I was all set to go. I just had to do the last step for the main dish. But the recipe said something about reducing the sauce. What did that mean? How do you do that? Okay, I panicked and picked up the telephone and ordered in."

Sound familiar? Small wonder. Cooking can be a perilous adventure. It doesn't help that so many recipes are written by cooking professionals who have forgotten the fear and anxiety of starting out. That's where I'M IN THE KITCHEN, NOW WHAT?! comes in. It is written by Pamela Richards, a cooking teacher for beginners, who knows how to dispel the anxiety most novice cooks feel upon entering the kitchen. Every recipe is broken down into steps and is written in simple, easy-to-follow language. Every recipe gives detailed instructions for procedures and techniques so that nothing is left to chance. Substitutions are right there. And every recipe anticipates every cook's questions. We're talking superlative driving instructions here! So crank up your stove and put on your mitts. There are some fabulous recipes waiting for you! Enjoy the journey.

Barb Chintz
Editorial Director, the Now What?!™ Series

contents

kitchen essentials

Having the right equipment on hand takes a huge amount of stress out of cooking. Here are the basics you will need to get started right.

EQUIPMENT

large saucepan

small saucepan

roasting pan

skillet

stockpot

Dutch oven

mixer

blender

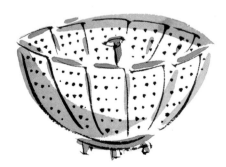

steamer

PREPARATION

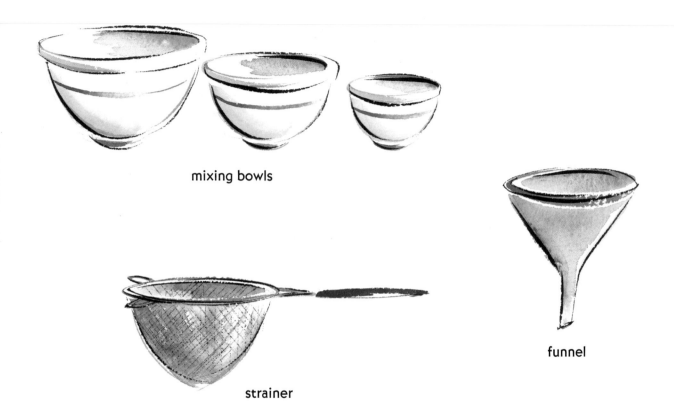

mixing bowls

strainer

funnel

colander

BAKING

pie pan

baking sheet

baking dish

MEASURES

measuring spoons

dry measures

measuring cup

TOOLS

tongs

spatula

rubber spatula

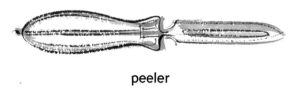

peeler

knives with knife sharpener

whisk

slotted spoons

wooden spoon

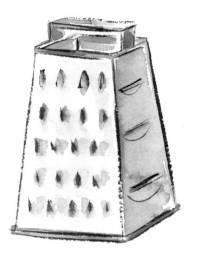

grater

pastry brush

1 Appetizers

Tempt your guests with these delicious offerings: Baked Spinach Balls (top), Guacamole (middle) and Cheese-Filled Phyllo Shells (bottom).

mushroom paté

A New Age paté, served chilled with a nice red wine—a Merlot or Pinot Noir—is sublime

Serves 6-8 ✳ *Prep time: 20 minutes* ✳ *Cooking time: 10 minutes*
✳ *Chilling time: 2 hours*

INGREDIENTS

- 4½ **tablespoons** butter, softened
- ½ **pound** mushrooms, cleaned and minced
- 1 **teaspoon** minced shallots
- 1 **teaspoon** minced garlic
- ¼ **cup** minced scallions
- ⅓ **cup** low-sodium chicken broth
- ¼ **cup** minced walnuts
- ½ **teaspoon** lemon juice
- 4 **ounces** light cream cheese, softened
- 1 **teaspoon** salt
- 1 **teaspoon** black pepper

1. MELT 2 tablespoons of butter in medium-sized skillet over medium heat. Add mushrooms, shallots, garlic and scallions and cook for 2 to 3 minutes, stirring occasionally.

2. ADD the chicken broth to the skillet and cook over medium heat until all the liquid has been absorbed, about 4 to 5 minutes. (It will bubble slightly.) Add the walnuts and lemon juice and stir to combine. Take the skillet off the stove and let mixture cool for about 20 minutes.

3. COMBINE cream cheese and remaining 2 ½ tablespoons of butter in a mixing bowl. Add the mushroom mixture and combine. Stir in salt and pepper and mix well.

4. FILL a 1-cup crockery bowl (or whatever pretty dish you have) with the mushroom mixture, and smooth surface. Cover with plastic wrap and refrigerate for at least two hours so flavors can meld.

5. SERVE with crackers or toast points (white toast cut into triangles) or for easy elegance—endive leaves.

easy bruschetta

Adding goat cheese and white beans accentuates this traditional Italian appetizer—fresh basil is key

Serves 8-10 ✳ *Prep time: 20 minutes* ✳ *Cooking time: 8 minutes*

INGREDIENTS

- **1 can** (15.5 ounces) small white beans, rinsed and drained
- **5** plum tomatoes, seeded and coasely chopped or 5 canned plum tomatoes, chopped
- **½ cup** minced onion
- **½ cup** fresh basil, rinsed and minced
- **3 cloves** garlic, minced
- **1 ½ tablespoons** balsamic vinegar
- **4 tablespoons** olive oil
- black pepper, to taste
- **1** long loaf Italian bread or French baguette, cut into ½-inch-thick slices
- **6 ounces** mild goat cheese, softened

1. PREHEAT oven to 375° F.

2. In a medium-sized mixing bowl, **COMBINE** white beans, tomatoes, onion, basil, garlic, balsamic vinegar and 2 tablespoons of the olive oil. Season with black pepper, to taste.

3. Place bread on large baking sheet and **BRUSH** with a pastry brush using the remaining 2 tablespoons of olive oil. (If you don't have a pastry brush, use the back of a spoon to smooth the oil over the bread.) **BAKE** until bread is toasted and golden brown, about 8 to 10 minutes. Watch the oven so bread doesn't burn!

4. REMOVE bread from the oven and spread the softened goat cheese over each bread slice. **TOP** with tomato-bean mixture.

5. SERVE immediately.

sun-dried tomatoes and cheese terrine

So pretty to look at, so scrumptious to eat when spread on crackers or pita bread

Serves 16 ✳ *Prep time: 20 minutes* ✳ *Cooking time: none*

INGREDIENTS

- **3 cups** grated Fontina cheese
- **12 ounces** reduced-fat cream cheese, softened
- **8 ounces** mild goat cheese
- **2 cups** prepared pesto or homemade (see page 140)
- **2 cups** sun-dried tomatoes, refreshed, drained and minced (see note)
- **1½ cups** pine nuts, lightly toasted

1. LINE a 9 x 5 x 3-inch **loaf pan** with plastic wrap, draping the wrap over the sides and ends of the pan. (It's just like lining a shoe box with tissue paper.)

2. SPREAD one cup of the Fontina cheese on bottom of prepared pan, covering entire surface.

3. In a small bowl, use a fork to **COMBINE** the cream cheese and goat cheese, mixing thoroughly.

4. SPREAD half of the cream cheese mixture over Fontina cheese layer.

5. SPREAD half of the pesto over cream cheese layer.

6. SPREAD half of the sun-dried tomatoes over pesto layer.

7. SPRINKLE half of the toasted pine nuts over tomato layer. Press down lightly with your hands.

8. SPRINKLE one cup Fontina over pine nuts.

9. REPEAT all layers, ending with a layer of Fontina cheese on top. Your loaf will be about 3 inches high.

10. FOLD plastic wrap over surface of cheese and cover pan with aluminum foil. Refrigerate terrine until ready to serve, or freeze for up to one month. To defrost, remove from freezer and let stand at room temperature for about 8 hours.

11. When ready to serve, **UNWRAP** top of loaf pan and invert the pan onto a platter. Lift pan up and remove foil and plastic wrap. Voilà, a gorgeous thing! Serve with crackers or pita bread, cut into small bite-sized triangles.

✳ NOW WHAT?! ✳

Ⓠ **Whenever I grate cheese with a grater, it always sticks to the grater. How do I avoid this mess?** Spray your grater with nonstick vegetable spray before grating cheese and the cleanup will be a breeze! If you are grating several foods, save messy foods like cheese for last. It also helps if you grate cheese when it's cold.

• • •

Ⓠ **What's the best way to clean cheese off my grater?** Use an old (but clean!) toothbrush for cleaning your grater— it's the perfect tool.

WHAT IS IT AND WHERE DO I FIND IT?

SUN-DRIED TOMATOES are usually dried in the sun, resulting in a chewy, intensely flavored, sweet, dark-red tomato. You can buy them dry, packed in oil, or in paste form. Dry-packed tomatoes are far less expensive than those packed in oil (it's the oil you are paying for!), and the only disadvantage is that they must be refreshed, or rehydrated before they can be used in a recipe. All you have to do to refresh the tomatoes is place them in a bowl, cover them with boiling water, and let them stand for about 15 minutes. Drain them and pat dry with paper towels before using.

• • •

FONTINA CHEESE is a semifirm cow's-milk cheese from Italy. It resembles a softer Gruyère, but has a richer taste.

• • •

PESTO is a wonderful herb sauce made from basil, pine nuts, olive oil, and Parmesan cheese. You can buy it already made. It's available in plastic containers in the specialty-food section of most supermarkets. To make your own, see page 140.

unfried chicken fingers

This is a super-quick, healthy appetizer that even little kids will devour

Yields 20 fingers ✳ *Prep time: 30 minutes* ✳ *Cooking time: 15 minutes*

INGREDIENTS

- **1 ½ pounds** skinless, boneless chicken breasts or chicken tenders
- **2 egg whites,** lightly beaten
- **1 ½ tablespoons** honey
- **2 ½ cups** crushed cornflakes
- **½ teaspoon** black pepper
- **1 teaspoon** garlic powder

SAUCE

- **⅓ cup** honey
- **3 tablespoons** Dijon mustard
- **4 ounces** apricot preserves
- **½ teaspoon** garlic powder
- **1 ½ teaspoons** soy sauce
- **¼ cup** water

for the chicken

1. PREHEAT oven to 450°F.

2. RINSE chicken and pat dry with paper towels. (This is vital, don't skip it.) Cut chicken into strips, 3 inches long by 3/4 inches wide, so they look like fingers. You should have about 20 to 25 strips.

3. COMBINE egg whites and honey in a small mixing bowl.

4. MIX crushed cornflakes, pepper, and garlic powder in a shallow bowl.

5. DIP chicken strips into the egg white mixture and then roll each strip in the crumb mixture to coat.

6. PLACE chicken fingers in a single layer on an ungreased baking sheet.

7. BAKE chicken in a 450°F oven for 12 to 15 minutes or

until juices run clear when pierced with a fork. Don't worry about turning them, it's not necessary.

for the sauce

1. In a medium-sized saucepan, **STIR** together the honey, mustard, apricot preserves, garlic powder, soy sauce, and water over medium-low heat. Cook until the preserves are just melted, stirring often for about 2 to 3 minutes. Transfer into a serving dish and serve as a dipping sauce for the chicken fingers. Or if you are short on time, use a prepared honey-mustard sauce.

❋ **NOW WHAT?!** ❋

I hate cutting up chicken. Is there an easy way? Yes. Use poultry shears or other all-purpose kitchen scissors to cut up chicken—they're often much easier to use than a knife; particularly a dull one!

• • •

Is raw chicken safe? I'm worried about salmonella. Bacteria! Bacteria! Bacteria! It flourishes in poultry at temperatures between 40°F and 140°F., so DO NOT let chicken sit out on your counter too long before cooking. Bacteria on raw poultry can contaminate other food it comes in contact with so it's vital that you always use hot, soapy water to thoroughly wash your hands, work surface, and utensils after preparing poultry.

FIRST PERSON DISASTER

Getting Plastered

I saw this great recipe for chicken and was really keen to try it. The recipe called for rolling the chicken pieces in flour and spices and then sautéeing it in chicken broth. What could be easier? Especially since a bag of flour was already there on the kitchen counter. I prepared the chicken and cooked them with some vegetables and called everyone in for dinner. There was only one problem—we couldn't cut into the chicken. It was as if it were encased in plaster. My son started to chuckle. "Mom, did you use the bag of plaster of Paris I left on the counter?" I nodded. "Didn't you always tell us to check your ingredients first?" I nodded again and added, "Remember, do I what I say, not what I do."

Sally M., New York, New York

nacho cheese dip

A creamy dip with just a dash of jalapeño; use tortilla chips to scoop it up—the secret is the beer

Serves 10 ✳ *Prep time: 15 minutes* ✳ *Cooking time: 10 minutes*

INGREDIENTS

- ¾ **cup** beer
- 1 ½ **teaspoons** ground cumin
- ½ **teaspoon** ground coriander
- 1 **teaspoon** dried oregano
- 1 **teaspoon** garlic powder
- 1 **can** (16 ounces) refried beans
- 1 ½ **cups** purchased salsa (medium or hot)
- 1 **teaspoon** minced canned or fresh jalapeño peppers
- 1 ½ **packages** (16 ounces each) Velveeta cheese, cut into 1-inch pieces
- 1 **tablespoon** dried cilantro or parsley or ½ **cup** chopped fresh cilantro

Tortilla chips

1. COMBINE beer, cumin, coriander, oregano, and garlic powder in a medium saucepan. Heat over low heat and bring to a simmer (you'll see pearl-sized bubbles forming). Add beans, salsa, and jalapeños and stir until heated through. Add Velveeta and stir until cheese melts, about 3-4 minutes. Stir in cilantro. Transfer to a bowl and serve with tortilla chips. Reheat as needed.

WHAT IS IT AND WHERE DO I FIND IT?

JALAPEÑO PEPPERS are small (2 to 3 inches long), but they are packed with hot spicy flavor. They are dark green and quite hot and are available fresh (look for them in the produce section of your supermarket) or canned, whole or already chopped. The more jalapeños you use, the spicier the dip!

* * *

VELVEETA CHEESE lets you relive the past with this dip. Yes, Velveeta is that orange stuff in the big rectangular box from days gone by. But it still makes a fabulous warm dipping sauce, smooth as velvet (hence the name) and better yet, it doesn't curdle (separate) when heated.

white bean hummus

Try white beans instead of chick peas for a sweeter, lighter "hummus"

Serves 10 ✳ *Prep time: 15 minutes* ✳ *Cooking time: none*

INGREDIENTS

- **1 can (15.5 ounces)** small white beans, rinsed and drained
- **3 tablespoons** lemon juice
- **¼ cup** chopped red onion, (about half an onion)
- **3 cloves** garlic, peeled
- **¼ teaspoon** ground cumin
- **¼ teaspoon** salt
- **½ teaspoon** black pepper
- **1 teaspoon** dried parsley or 2 tablespoons chopped fresh parsley

Pita bread triangles

Mini carrots, raw

1. PLACE everything except the parsley, pita bread, and carrots in a blender or the bowl of food processor fitted with a steel blade; process until smooth. Spoon the hummus into a serving bowl and garnish with chopped parsley.

2. SERVE with pita triangles and raw carrots.

✳ NOW WHAT?! ✳

Why do I have to rinse and drain the beans? Is there something wrong with the juices in the can?

No. It's just that those juices are loaded with salt. You need to rinse them off or the taste of your recipe will be distorted.

baked spinach balls

A delicious and healthful way to start a party

Serves 6 ✳ *Prep time: 15 minutes* ✳ *Cooking time: 12 minutes*

INGREDIENTS

- **1 box (10 ounces)** frozen chopped spinach
- **¼ cup** minced shallots
- **2** extra large **egg whites,** lightly beaten
- **½ cup** plain bread crumbs
- **¼ cup** plus 2 tablespoons grated Parmesan cheese
- **1 ½ tablespoons** lemon juice
- **½ teaspoon** salt
- **½ teaspoon** black pepper

YOGURT DIP

- **½ cup** plain low-fat yogurt
- **1 teaspoon** dried dill or 3 teaspoons chopped fresh dill
- **1 ½ teaspoons** garlic paste or 1 teaspoon garlic powder

1. PREHEAT oven to 400° F.

2. MICROWAVE spinach according to package instructions. Drain spinach, cool, and wring it dry (see amazing tip on the next page).

3. COMBINE the spinach, shallots, egg whites, bread crumbs, Parmesan, lemon juice, salt, and pepper in a medium-sized bowl.

4. ROLL the spinach mixture into 1-inch balls. How? Just put a little in your hand and roll into a ball as you would clay. Place the balls on a baking sheet that has been sprayed with vegetable cooking spray. Bake on the middle rack of your oven for 12 minutes. They should be slightly golden brown. Serve immediately with yogurt dip on the side.

for the Dip

1. COMBINE the yogurt, dill, and garlic in a small bowl, mixing well with a fork.

2. SERVE the spinach balls with the dip.

Bite-sized morsels of spinach with a refreshing yogurt-dill dip.

How do I dry spinach?

The best way to squeeze all the water out of spinach is to place it in a clean dish towel or, believe it or not, into the foot of a clean knee-hi stocking and wring dry. You'll spend too much time and effort trying to get the water out using any other method!

guacamole

Avocados and a fabulous blend of spices and garlic make a superb guacamole every time

Serves 6-8 ✳ *Prep time: 15 minutes* ✳ *Cooking time: None*

INGREDIENTS

- **4** ripe Haas avocados
- **3 tablespoons** lemon juice
- **3 tablespoons** lime juice
- **1** large tomato, seeded and minced
- **¼ cup** onion, minced
- **2 cloves** garlic, minced
- **2 teaspoons** black pepper
- **1 teaspoon** salt
- **5-10 dashes** Tabasco
- **1 ½ teaspoons** dried cilantro or **2 tablespoons** chopped fresh cilantro
- **Large** bag of tortilla chips

1. SLICE each avocado in half; remove and discard the pits. Using a large spoon, scoop the meat into a medium-sized bowl. Add the lemon and lime juices.

2. MASH avocado with back side of a fork until slightly chunky, mixing it with the lemon and lime juices.

3. CUT the tomato in quarters and use a fork to dig out the seeds. Chop the tomato into ¼-inch pieces.

4. ADD tomato and the rest of the ingredients to the avocado mixture and mix until just combined. Makes about 3 cups.

5. SERVE with tortilla chips.

WHAT IS IT AND WHERE DO I FIND IT?

HAAS AVOCADO Once upon a time there was an alligator pear, better known as the Haas avocado we love today. True, it looks ugly and bumpy on the outside, but its flesh is buttery and irresistible! The other variety that you also see in the market, which has shiny skin and far less flavor, is known as the Fuerte.

How do I keep avocados, and hence guacamole, green?

The flesh of avocados is a lovely shade of green, however it turns brown when exposed to air. To retard browning, brush the surface with lemon or lime juice. The faster you add lemon or lime juice to your guacamole, the less likely it is that it will turn brown. It's the acid in the juice that slows the browning and brightens the flavor. Once you have combined all of the ingredients, press plastic wrap directly onto the dip (as in touching it) and this will help maintain its color.

• • •

How do I know if my avocado is ripe?

By the time most people have finished testing for ripeness, the avocado is so bruised that it's no longer worth using any more! To check for ripeness, hold the fruit in your hand. If it yields slightly to gentle pressure from your palm, it is ripe. In other words, if it gives a little, it's ready for consumption. Be careful not to squeeze it too much as you'll induce bad spots. If its hard, take it home and wait a few days till it ripens. If you're in a hurry, save a day by wrapping it in aluminum foil. (Microwaving will not ripen it, just soften it.)

Nothing disappears
faster than flavorful,
homemade guacamole.

spinach dip

Sure, onion dip is fine, but why not try something
a little more elegant? No cooking required.

Serves 6 ✳ *Prep time: 10 minutes* ✳ *Cooking time: None*

INGREDIENTS

1	large round peasant bread
⅓	**cup** extra-virgin olive oil
2	**boxes (10 ounces each)** frozen spinach, thawed and drained
2½	**tablespoons** lemon juice
3	**cloves** garlic, chopped

salt and black pepper to taste

1. CUT a ½-inch-thick slice of bread and place it on a plate.
Pour 3 tablespoons olive oil over it, turning to coat completely. Let bread stand in the oil until absorbed (about 5
minutes) and then tear bread into pieces.

2. In a blender or the bowl of a food processor fitted with a
steel blade, **ADD** the spinach and blend until smooth. Add
the bread, lemon juice, and garlic and blend or process until
smooth. Add remaining olive oil, and purée the mixture.
Season with salt and pepper, and spoon into a bowl. Dip will
be runny. Serve with thin slices of warm crusty peasant
bread or crackers.

✳ **WHAT IS IT? WHERE DO I FIND IT?** ✳

PEASANT BREAD is the down-home name for any round loaf of white
bread that is crusty on the outside. They are anywhere from 5 to 10
inches in diameter and are available at large supermarkets, specialty
food shops, or bakeries.

cheese and bacon puffs

These are great with serious cocktails or a lovely chilled Chardonnay

Yields 30 puffs ✴ *Prep time: 15 minutes* ✴ *Cooking time: 10 minutes*

INGREDIENTS

- **1 pound** cooked, crisp bacon, crumbled
- **1 cup** mayonnaise
- **1 cup** grated sharp cheddar cheese
- **4 scallions**, sliced thin (white and green parts)
- **2 tablespoons** dry sherry
- **1 teaspoon** white Worcestershire sauce (optional)
- **3 drops** Tabasco (or other hot sauce)
- Melba rounds

1. **FRY** the bacon in a skillet or cook it in a microwave until crisp; crisp bacon crumbles more easily. (To microwave: separate the strips and place 6 at a time on a paper towel. Roll up the paper towel and place in the microwave and cook for 2 to 3 minutes on high. Continue with another set of strips on a new piece of towel.) Set bacon aside so it can cool, overnight if you wish, then chop the bacon into ¼-inch pieces or crumble it with your fingers.

2. **MIX** all ingredients in a bowl and chill for 3 hours or overnight. (It will keep for as long as three days, refrigerated, if you want to make it ahead of time).

When Ready to Serve

3. **PREHEAT** broiler. Make sure the oven's upper rack is about 5 inches from the broiler coils before you turn it on.

4. **SPREAD** mixture on melba rounds and place on a cookie sheet. Put the cookie sheet on the oven rack and broil until the cheese is bubbly, only 2 to 3 minutes.

5. **SERVE** immediately.

cheese-filled phyllo shells

Ready-made phyllo shells are so easy to use in this sumptuous appetizer

Yields 45 ✳ *Prep time: 20 minutes* ✳ *Cooking time: 10 minutes*

INGREDIENTS

- **3** boxes frozen phyllo shells
- ⅔ **cup** grated Parmesan cheese
- ½ **pound** mozzarella cheese, grated
- ¾ **pound** light cream cheese, softened
- **2** eggs, lightly beaten
- **I cup** refreshed sun-dried tomatoes, chopped (see page 17)
- **I cup** fresh basil leaves, washed, dried and minced or 2 tablespoons dried basil
- **3 cloves** garlic, minced
- Salt and black pepper to taste

I. PREHEAT oven to 350°F. Remove the phyllo shells from their boxes and place on an ungreased baking or cookie sheet. Shells will thaw in about 10 minutes.

2. MIX together cheeses, eggs, tomatoes, basil, garlic, salt, and pepper in large bowl.

3. FILL each phyllo shell with mixture, mounding slightly.

4. BAKE in oven for 8 to 10 minutes, or until mixture begins to bubble. Remove shells from baking sheet and place on serving platter and serve warm.

WHAT IS IT? WHERE DO I FIND IT?

PHYLLO SHELLS come fifteen to a box and are available in the freezer section of most grocery stores. They should be near the frozen pie crusts and phyllo sheets.

Phyllo shells (shown cooked, inset above) turn an ordinary filling of cheese and sun-dried tomatoes into an elegant treat.

2 Soups

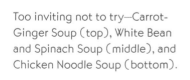

Too inviting not to try—Carrot-Ginger Soup (top), White Bean and Spinach Soup (middle), and Chicken Noodle Soup (bottom).

chicken noodle soup

Put leftover chicken to good use with this delicious, hearty soup

Serves 6 ✳ *Prep time: 20 minutes* ✳ *Cooking time: 35 minutes*

INGREDIENTS

- **1 teaspoon** olive oil
- **1 cup** chopped onion
- **1 ½ teaspoons** dried oregano
- **1 teaspoon** dried basil
- **2 cloves** garlic, minced
- **8 cups** low-sodium chicken stock (canned or homemade, (see page 50)
- **1 cup** peeled, diced potato
- **1 ½ cups** chopped celery
- **1 ½ cups** sliced carrots
- **3 ½ cups** shredded cooked chicken (white meat only)
- **2 boxes (10 ounces each)** frozen chopped spinach, thawed and drained
- **1 ¼ teaspoons** salt
- **1-2 teaspoons** black pepper
- **6 ounces** uncooked egg noodles (thin ones)
- **2 tablespoons** all-purpose flour

1. **HEAT** the oil in a large heavy soup pot over medium heat.

2. **ADD** the onion and cook over medium-high heat (turning the onions frequently so they won't burn) for about 3 minutes, or until they are translucent.

3. **ADD** the oregano, basil, and garlic and sauté 1 minute. (Cooking the herbs in oil brings out more of their flavor.)

4. **ADD** 7½ cups of the chicken stock. Increase the heat, bringing the mixture to a **BOIL** (nickel-sized bubbles will form every few seconds); add the potato.

5. **REDUCE** the heat and **SIMMER** (pearl-sized bubbles will form every few seconds). Cook for 15 minutes, uncovered, stirring occasionally.

6. Using a potato masher or the back of large spoon, **MASH** the potato into the stock. The soup should look a little cloudy. (This is the trick to thickening the soup).

7. **ADD** the celery, carrots, chicken, spinach, salt, and pepper and return to a boil. Reduce the heat and simmer 5 to 6 minutes.

8. ADD the noodles, return to a boil and cook 5 minutes, or until the noodles are tender.

9. While the noodles are cooking, **WHISK** together ½ cup stock and flour in a small bowl. (This mixture is called a roux. It looks a bit like goopy wallpaper paste but its purpose is quite elegant: it slightly thickens the soup.) Whisk several tablespoonsful of the soup's broth into the roux, then stir the mixture into the soup. Simmer for 3 to 4 minutes.

10. LADLE the soup into warmed bowls and serve.

✳ **NOW WHAT?!** ✳

Q What's the best way to avoid adding too much salt or pepper?

Add both salt and pepper gradually, about ½ teaspoon at a time, tasting as you go.

• • •

Q What should I do if I add too much salt?

Add a peeled, thinly sliced raw potato to the pot and simmer the soup for 10 to 15 minutes. Remove the potato before serving the soup.

down east clam chowder

The real deal—the clams in their shells in the soup

Serves 6 ✳ *Prep time: 20 minutes* ✳ *Cooking time: 30 minutes*

INGREDIENTS

3 tablespoons butter

4 small leeks, washed and thinly sliced

2 cloves garlic, minced

¼ cup flour

3 cups whole milk

3 bottles (8 ounces each) clam juice

1 ⅔ pounds russet potatoes, peeled and cut into ½-inch cubes

1 tablespoon black pepper

salt to taste

4 ½ pounds fresh littleneck clams, the shells well scrubbed, or 3 cans (8 ounces each)

1. In a large, heavy pot **MELT** the butter over medium heat just until liquid, but not yet turning brown. Add the leeks and garlic and cook over medium-high heat for 3 minutes, turning the mixture frequently so it won't burn.

2. ADD the flour and stir with a spoon to combine for about 2 minutes.

3. Gradually **MIX** in the milk and clam juice, preferably with a whisk.

4. INCREASE the heat to high, bringing the mixture to a boil (nickel-sized bubbles will form every few seconds). Add the potatoes.

5. REDUCE the heat to low and cook soup, uncovered, for about 15 minutes, stirring occasionally. Season to taste with salt and pepper.

6. ADD the clams in their shells. Simmer for 4–5 minutes more, or until the clams open.

7. LADLE the chowder into bowls and serve.

🅠 **Whenever I make chowder, my clams get tough. Why does this happen?**

The key to chowder is not to cook it too long; the flavors get too strong, and the clams toughen up. If you remove the soup from the heat promptly just when the clams open, the resulting flavors will be gentle, and the clams will remain tender.

• • •

🅠 **How do I tell if a clam is bad?**

When you select clams, make sure the shells are tightly closed. If they appear slightly open, give them a rap with your knuckles. If they don't close up, toss them out. They are either dead or dying.

• • •

🅠 **Can I use canned clams for this recipe?**

Yes, but the texture of canned clams will be different from fresh ones. You will need 1½ pounds of canned clams or 3 cans (8 ounces each).

• • •

🅠 **How do I eat the clams in the soup?**

Some of the clams will fall out of their shells and into the soup. Some will fall out after they have been ladled into bowls. Eat those with your spoon. The ones that remain in their shells will require a little effort. Scoop out a clam shell with a spoon and use your fingers to dig it out. Who said you shouldn't eat with your fingers?

sherried mushroom soup

A silky, flavorful first course or light supper with bread and salad

Serves 6 ✳ *Prep time: 15 minutes* ✳ *Cooking time: 35 minutes*

INGREDIENTS

- **3 tablespoons** butter
- **1 ¼ cups** chopped onion
- **2 ½ pounds** portobello and shiitake mushrooms, thinly sliced (see note)
- **5 cups** low-sodium chicken broth (canned or homemade, see page 50)
- **⅓ cup** dry sherry (see note)
- Salt and black pepper
- **¼ cup** heavy cream or evaporated skim milk

1. In a large heavy saucepan, **MELT** the butter over medium heat until it is liquid and not yet turning brown.

2. **ADD** the onions and cook over medium-high heat for 5 minutes, turning frequently.

3. **ADD** the mushrooms and cook for about 8 to 10 minutes, until the mushrooms have softened and the liquid they give off has evaporated.

4. **ADD** the chicken broth. Reduce the heat and simmer uncovered (pearl-sized bubbles will form every few seconds) for 15 minutes.

5. **REMOVE** the soup from the heat and allow it to cool for 5 minutes. Pour half the soup into a blender and purée. Pour the puréed mixture back into the chunky portion of soup.

6. **ADD** the sherry, salt and pepper and cream; stir to combine. Heat the soup gradually for a few minutes until it's hot, stirring constantly to prevent curdling (see page 37).

7. **LADLE** the soup into bowls and serve.

☀ NOW WHAT?! ☀

 Why does cream curdle?

If cream is poured too quickly into a very hot mixture, or if it is heated too quickly, the protein in the cream cooks, forming solid lumps, or curds, that separate from the watery whey. Curdling can be prevented by heating the cream slowly or by gradually mixing in a little of the hot liquid to the cream before adding it to a heated mixture.

• • •

 Why do my mushrooms always become mushy after I wash them?

Clean mushrooms just before you cook them. Never immerse them in water; mushrooms are extremely absorbent (much like a sponge) and will become mushy. The best solution is to rinse them in a colander under cold running water and then immediately blot them dry with a paper towel.

• • •

Is it necessary to sauté the mushrooms before making the soup?

Yes, sautéing mushrooms concentrates and releases their flavor. Don't crowd them all into the pan—you want to be able to stir them around. If the temperature is not hot enough or if the mushrooms are crowded, they will steam instead of sauté, and will not be as flavorful.

WHAT IS IT? WHERE DO I FIND IT?

MUSHROOMS come in many varieties and most are available in grocery stores. If the large brown portobello or the Japanese black shiitake are not available in your store, ask for chanterelle, morel, or porcini mushrooms. Look for the firm, straight gills that indicate a mushroom is fresh. Remove the large stems of the mushrooms for this recipe. Use mushrooms soon after purchase, they don't keep well past 4 days.

• • •

SHERRY is a fortified wine. It comes in three styles: dry, sweet, or cream. For cooking purposes, get a good dry sherry, such as Amontillado. It will add tremendous flavor to food. Once opened, a bottle of sherry will keep for up to one year.

carrot-ginger soup

The zippy tang of fresh ginger combines with the sweetness of carrots to create a superb soup

Serves 6 ✳ *Prep time: 20 minutes* ✳ *Cooking time: 25 minutes*

INGREDIENTS

- **3 tablespoons** vegetable oil
- **2** leeks, washed and minced (white parts only)
- **¼ cup** peeled, minced fresh ginger, or 1 tablespoon ground ginger
- **4 cups** low-sodium chicken broth (canned or homemade, see page 50)
- **1 ½ pounds** carrots, peeled and sliced (about 4 cups)
- **1 cup** orange juice
- **½ cup** half-and-half
- **½ teaspoon** ground cinnamon
- **½ teaspoon** ground cardamom
- **1 teaspoon** salt
- **1 ¼ teaspoons** black pepper
- **Garnish** (optional): chopped fresh parsley

1. HEAT the oil in a large, heavy saucepan. Add the leeks and ginger and cook on medium-high heat, turning the mixture frequently so it won't burn, for about 5 minutes.

2. ADD chicken broth and carrots. Increase the heat to high and bring the mixture to a **BOIL** (nickel-sized bubbles will form every few seconds). Reduce the heat to low so that the mixture **SIMMERS** (pearl-sized bubbles will form every few seconds). Cover the pot and cook until the carrots are tender, about 20 minutes.

3. REMOVE the soup from the heat and let it stand for five minutes. Then purée the soup in batches in a blender. Return the puréed mixture to the saucepan.

4. STIR in the orange juice, half-and-half, cinnamon, cardamom, salt, and pepper and simmer uncovered for 5 minutes.

5. LADLE the soup into bowls, garnish with parsley (if desired), and serve.

☀ NOW WHAT?! ☀

Why do I have to bring the soup to a boil first, then immediately lower the heat and simmer?

The initial boiling helps bring out the flavors. Simmering the soup afterwards does not reduce the liquid, but simply finishes the cooking process.

WHAT IS IT? WHERE DO I FIND IT?

GINGER is a knobby root vegetable that can be found in the produce section of most supermarkets. Buy only smooth, spicy-smelling ginger; if it is cracked or wrinkled, it's past its prime. Use a vegetable peeler to remove the thin, brown skin—but be sure to peel just the skin as the delicate flesh just under the surface is the most flavorful.

Carrot-ginger soup served with hot crusty bread is the perfect meal on a cool autumn day.

butternut squash soup

A true fall classic, earthy-flavored and golden-hued

Serves 4-6 ✳ *Prep time: 15 minutes* ✳ *Cooking time: 30 minutes*

INGREDIENTS

- **4 tablespoons** butter
- **1 tablespoon** vegetable oil
- **1 medium** Spanish onion, chopped
- **1** leek, washed and minced (white and light-green part, only)
- **2 pounds** butternut squash, peeled, seeded and cut into 1-inch pieces
- **4-5 cups** low-sodium chicken broth (canned or homemade, see page 50)
- **¼ teaspoon** ground nutmeg
- **1 teaspoon** salt
- **1 teaspoon** black pepper
- **⅓ cup** evaporated skim milk
- **Garnish** (optional): Fresh parsley or dill, chopped or dried

1. In a heavy large saucepan **MELT** the butter over medium heat for about 2 minutes until it's liquid but not yet turning brown. Add the oil to the butter and stir together with a whisk or spoon.

2. **ADD** the onion and leek and cook over medium-high heat for 5 to 6 minutes, turning the onions frequently so they don't burn.

3. **ADD** the squash and cook 5 minutes.

4. **ADD** 4 cups of broth and the nutmeg to the pot. Reduce the heat to medium-low and **simmer** (pearl-sized bubbles will form every few seconds) for 15 to 20 minutes or until the squash is tender enough to pierce with a fork.

5. **REMOVE** the soup from the heat and let it cool for 5 minutes. Purée the soup in batches in a blender. Return the soup to the saucepan and stir in the salt, pepper, and evaporated milk. (If soup is too thick, thin it by adding more broth, a few extra tablespoons at a time. Rewarm the soup on low heat and taste it for seasoning—add salt and pepper as you wish.)

6. LADLE the soup into individual bowls and garnish with parsley or dill. Serve

WHAT IS IT? WHERE DO I FIND IT?

BUTTERNUT SQUASH is a winter squash 6 to 9 inches tall with a bulbous base and hard, light-brown skin. Before cooking, cut it in half and discard the seeds in the center. To make peeling the skin easier, microwave the squash on HIGH for 1 to 2 minutes, then let it stand for a few minutes longer. Use a sharp knife or vegetable peeler to remove the skin.

* * *

EVAPORATED MILK. Think of it as thick milk in a can. Essentially, it's regular milk with about 60 percent of the water removed. It's a cook's secret weapon: just open and pour it into dishes that require cream—creamed soups, vegetables in cream sauce, gravies. Evaporated milk comes in whole, low-fat, and skimmed versions. It's sold in cans and, unlike sweetened condensed milk, is not sweet. You can find it in the baking section at the supermarket. Keep a few cans in the pantry—they come in handy for enriching last-minute meals.

✳ NOW WHAT?! ✳

Can I use sweetened condensed milk instead of evaporated milk?
No! It would not work. Sweetened condensed milk is about 40 percent sugar; the sweetness would ruin the earthy flavor of the soup. Evaporated milk is not sweetened.

turkey and black bean soup

Turn leftover turkey into a fiesta!

Serves 6 ✸ *Prep time: 20 minutes* ✸ *Cooking time: 45 minutes*

INGREDIENTS

- **2 tablespoons** canola or vegetable oil
- **1 ¼ cups** chopped red onion
- **1 ¼ cups** chopped carrot
- **1 cup** chopped celery
- **4 cloves** garlic, minced
- **1 ½ tablespoons** ground cumin
- **1 teaspoon** dried oregano
- **½ teaspoon** dried coriander
- **4 cups** low-sodium chicken broth (canned or homemade, see page 50)
- **2 ¼ cups** water
- **1 teaspoon** salt
- **2 cans** (15.5 ounces each) black beans, drained
- **1 pound** turkey breasts, cooked and coarsely chopped
- **1** red bell pepper, cut into ½-inch pieces
- **2 teaspoons** dried cilantro
- **¼ cup** dry sherry (see page 37)

1. HEAT the oil in a large pot over medium heat. Add the onion, carrot, celery, garlic, cumin, oregano, and coriander; cook over medium heat for 5 minutes, stirring constantly so the food doesn't burn.

2. ADD the broth, water, salt, and beans and stir to combine. Increase the heat to high and bring the mixture to a **BOIL** (nickel-sized bubbles will form every few seconds). Reduce the heat to low so that the mixture **SIMMERS** (pearl-sized bubbles will form every few seconds). Cook for 20 to 25 minutes, or until vegetables are just tender enough to be pierced with a fork.

3. REMOVE the bean mixture from the heat and let it cool for 10 minutes. Transfer half of the bean mixture to a blender and purée until smooth. Return the purée to the remaining chunky bean mixture and stir to combine.

4. ADD the cooked turkey. Stir in the bell pepper, cilantro, and sherry. Cook the mixture for 5 minutes over medium-low heat, stirring, until thoroughly heated.

5. LADLE the soup into bowls and serve.

Storage tip: This soup can be frozen in an airtight plastic container for up to three months (after that, the texture begins to degrade). To thaw soup, reheat it over medium-low heat, stirring frequently.

WHAT IS IT AND WHERE DO I FIND IT?

BLACK BEANS, also known as frijoles negros or turtle beans, are a staple of Mexican, Caribbean, and Central and South American cuisines. They are more flavorful than most other beans and, like all beans, are high in soluble fiber and are a good source of fat-free protein.

* * *

COOKED TURKEY Use leftovers, or buy turkey already cooked and diced (look in the meat section of your grocery store). Or cook ground turkey, then add to the soup.

FIRST PERSON DISASTER

Go soak your beans

I thought it would be great to use the beans that come in plastic bags instead of the ones in cans. They look so authentic. I emptied the bag into the soup pot and cooked the soup according to the recipe. Imagine my surprise when I tried a spoonful and cracked a tooth because those beans were still really hard.

Later, a friend who's an experienced cook explained that the beans in the cans are already cooked, and only need heating up, but the dried beans in the bags are not. She told me how to soak the dried ones overnight and then simmer them slowly until they are tender. Now I use either dried beans or canned, depending on how much time I have. And the money I save by using dried beans just might pay for my dental bill in, oh, say, 50 years.

Geoffrey L., Avon, Connecticut

gazpacho

All the best of summer in a bowl—with no cooking! Make it zesty (spicy hot) or mild, as you wish

Serves 8-10 ✴ *Prep time: 20 minutes* ✴ *Cooking time: none* ✴ *Chilling time: 1 hour*

INGREDIENTS

10	tomatoes
2	cucumbers, seeds removed or 2 seedless cucumbers (see next page)
2	red bell peppers, cored and seeded
1	yellow bell pepper, cored and seeded
2	red onions, peeled
6	**cloves** garlic, minced
⅓	**cup** white wine vinegar
3	**teaspoons** lime juice
4	**cups** Sacramento tomato juice
¾	**cup** chopped fresh basil
4	**tablespoons** olive oil
½	**teaspoon** Tabasco
1¼	**teaspoons** salt
2	**teaspoons** black pepper

1. **CUT** the tomatoes, cucumbers, bell peppers, and onions into 1-inch chunks. Don't mix them together yet.

2. **PLACE** each vegetable *separately* into the blender or in the bowl of a food processor fitted with a steel blade, and pulse until it is just coarsely chopped. Be careful not to over-chop; you want some texture.

3. **TRANSFER** vegetables to a large bowl.

4. **ADD** the garlic, vinegar, lime juice, tomato juice, basil, olive oil, Tabasco, salt, and pepper to vegetables. Mix well, using a large spoon and refrigerate for at least an hour, or longer. (The longer gazpacho sits, the more its flavors develop.)

5. **LADLE** the soup into bowls or mugs, and garnish with sprigs of dill if you like.

WHAT IS IT AND WHERE DO I FIND IT?

SEEDLESS CUCUMBERS are also referred to as English seedless or hot-house cucumbers. They are quite long and thin and are usually sold individually wrapped. They are sweeter than traditional cucumbers and are not covered with a waxy finish to preserve them, so you don't have to peel them.

* * *

SACRAMENTO TOMATO JUICE This brand of tomato juice has a tremendous amount of flavor that enhances the soup, so try to use it if possible. You will find it in your supermarket.

✳ **NOW WHAT?!** ✳

🔵 **Can I serve gazpacho warm?**
Yes. You can serve it at room temperature, but its flavors are most pronounced if it is served cold.

* * *

🔵 **What wine do you serve with it?**
Try a nice dry Sauvignon Blanc or Fumé Blanc.

zucchini soup

Wondering what to do with all that zucchini from the garden? Try this easy summer soup

Serves 4-6 ✳ *Prep time: 10 minutes* ✳ *Cooking time: 20 minutes*

INGREDIENTS

- **2 tablespoons** olive oil
- **1 large** onion, chopped
- **2 cloves** garlic, minced
- **6 cups** grated zucchini
- **4 cups** low-sodium chicken broth (canned or homemade, see page 50)
- **2 teaspoons each** dried flat-leaf parsley, chives, thyme, basil, and dill or 3 tablespoons each of fresh

salt and black pepper to taste

Garnish (optional): low-fat yogurt or grated Parmesan cheese

1. HEAT the oil in a large saucepan over medium heat.

2. ADD the onion and garlic and **sauté** (cook over medium heat, turning the food frequently so it won't burn) for 3 minutes. Stir in the zucchini and cook for 5 more minutes.

3. ADD chicken broth, and increase the heat until the mixture **BOILS** (nickel-sized bubbles will form every few seconds). Reduce the heat to low and **SIMMER** (pearl-sized bubbles will form every few seconds) uncovered for 10 minutes.

4. REMOVE soup from the heat and let it cool for 5 to 10 minutes. Add the herbs and the salt and pepper, stirring well. Taste and add more seasonings if needed.

5. POUR the cooled soup into a blender or a food processor fitted with a steel blade. Blend the soup until it is quite smooth, return to the saucepan and reheat.

6. LADLE the soup into bowls and garnish with a dollop of low-fat yogurt or a sprinkling of grated Parmesan cheese.

Q **How do I grate zucchini without scraping my knuckles?**

While you are grating, hold the zucchini bottom-end up with your fin-
gertips. When the zucchini gets short, press it down with the flat of
your palm as you drag it back and forth across the grater. (If you have
a food processor, use that instead, fitted with the grating disc.)

• • •

Q **The last time I poured something hot into my blender the glass container
cracked. What happened?**

The most likely explanation is that the container was made of untempered, rather than tempered, glass. Tempered glass can withstand sud-
den changes in temperature. Untempered glass requires that the food
be cooled—or added slowly to the container so that the glass is
warmed gradually—before blending.

white bean and spinach soup

This main-dish soup warms your soul on a cold winter day—you'll make it over and over again

Serves 6-8 ✳ *Prep time: 25 minutes* ✳ *Cooking time: 35 minutes*

INGREDIENTS

- **2 cans** (15.5 ounces each) small white beans
- **3 tablespoons** olive oil
- **1 large** onion, chopped
- **¾ pound** peeled baby carrots, chopped into ½-inch bits
- **3 stalks** of celery, washed and chopped into ½-inch slices
- **6 cups** low-sodium chicken broth (canned or homemade, see page 50)
- **8 cloves** garlic, peeled and minced
- **1** bay leaf
- **1 teaspoon** dried rosemary, crumbled
- **1 teaspoon** salt or to taste
- **1 teaspoon** celery seed
- **2 teaspoons** black pepper
- **¼ teaspoon** red pepper flakes
- **2 boxes** (10 ounces each) chopped spinach, thawed

1. PLACE the beans in a colander and rinse with cold water. Drain them thoroughly and set them aside in a small bowl.

2. In a 6-quart soup pot **HEAT** the oil over medium heat for 1 minute. Add chopped onion and **sauté** (stirring frequently so the onions won't burn) for about 5 minutes.

3. ADD the carrots and celery, and sauté for 5 minutes more.

4. ADD the beans, chicken broth, garlic, bay leaf, and rosemary. Reduce the heat to low and **SIMMER** (pearl-sized bubbles will form every few seconds) for 20 minutes.

5. REMOVE the bay leaf (it adds wonderful flavor to foods, but is not enjoyable to chew).

6. ADD the salt, celery seed, black pepper, and red pepper flakes. Cook for an additional 5 minutes. Taste for seasoning, add salt or pepper as you wish.

7. REMOVE the soup from the heat and let it cool for about 5 minutes. Pour half of the soup into a blender and blend about 30 seconds, until the mixture is smooth. Return the puréed portion to the chunky soup in the pot and stir to combine.

8. STIR in the spinach. Cook for 1 minute more.

8. LADLE the soup into bowls.

For a hearty meal, accompany soup with a green salad and warm sourdough or French bread.

chicken stock

Homemade stock—the secret that separates good soups from great ones—use it whenever a recipe calls for chicken broth

Yields 10 to 12 cups ✳ *Prep time: 20 minutes* ✳ *Cooking time: 3 hours*

INGREDIENTS

- **3 pounds** chicken bones, wings, necks, backs, skin (and giblets, if available)
- **2** onions, unpeeled and quartered
- **2 celery ribs**, cut into 2-inch pieces
- **2** carrots, cut into 2-inch pieces
- **2** leeks, washed and chopped
- **4 cloves** garlic, unpeeled
- **1** bay leaf
- **1 sprig** fresh thyme
- **5 sprigs** fresh parsley
- **10** black peppercorns or **2 teaspoons** black pepper

salt as desired

- **16 cups** cold water (or enough to cover ingredients)

1. PLACE all the ingredients in a large (at least 6-quart) stockpot. Bring mixture to a **boil** (nickel-sized bubbles will form every few seconds) and cook for 10 minutes. You will see some dark foam forming on the surface. Skim that off with a spoon.

2. REDUCE the heat and **simmer** (pearl-sized bubbles will form every few seconds) uncovered for 2 to 3 hours, skimming foam from the top occasionally.

3. SCOOP out the chicken with a slotted spoon and discard it. Allow the soup to cool slightly.

4. POUR the stock through a large, fine-meshed sieve or strainer into a large **heatproof** bowl (one that doesn't conduct heat; try glass or ceramic, not metal) that you've placed in a sink. Take care not to splash yourself when pouring the hot liquid through the sieve.

5. PRESS the bones and vegetables remaining in the strainer with the spoon until all the broth is released, then discard them. If you have time, chill the stock in the refrigerator and remove any fat that rises to the surface.

◉ How do I get rid of the fat fast?

You can use a fat-separator cup—an inexpensive and useful cup made of plastic or glass with a spout at the base. When you pour the stock out of this cup, the fat stays behind—magical! Another way is to use a heavy zip-top plastic bag. Let the stock cool, then pour the stock into the bag and seal it. Put the bag in the refrigerator and prop it up so that the zip-top is at the top. Let it stand in the refrigerator. When the fat has risen to the top (about 10 minutes), snip off a bottom corner of the bag and drain the stock into a container, stopping before the fat reaches the opening. Discard the bag and the fat—a neat trick!

• • •

◉ How do I freeze chicken stock and for how long?

You can freeze it in freezer-proof zip-lock bags— 2 cups per bag. Or you can freeze larger amounts in an airtight plastic container. Chicken stock can be frozen for up to 6 months.

Salads

New Wave Spinach Salad (top), Vegetable Couscous Salad (middle), and Wild Rice Salad (bottom) can be either a light main course or side dish.

classic coleslaw

This is a traditional coleslaw—if you have a food processor to do the slicing, it's incredibly quick

Serves 6-8 ✳ *Prep time: 15 minutes* ✳ *Cooking time: none*

INGREDIENTS

- ½ **head** red cabbage (about 1 pound)
- ½ **head** green or white cabbage (about 1 pound)
- 4 large carrots, peeled (or 3 cups packaged shredded carrots)
- 2 **cups** light mayonnaise
- ¼ **cup** Dijon mustard
- 1 **tablespoon** lime juice
- 2 **teaspoons** sugar
- 2 **tablespoons** white vinegar or red wine vinegar
- 2 **teaspoons** celery seeds
- 1½ **teaspoons** celery salt
- 1½ **teaspoons** black pepper

1. CUT the cabbages into wedges and feed them into a food processor fitted with a thick slicing blade. Process cabbage in batches and transfer to a large bowl. They can also be sliced into thin strips with a sharp kitchen knife.

2. SWITCH over to the food processor's grating blade. Cut carrots in thirds and feed them in horizontally so you'll end up with long shreds. Process in batches and mix into bowl with cabbage. Or use that knife again.

3. In a medium bowl, **WHISK** together all remaining ingredients to make dressing.

4. POUR enough dressing over grated vegetables to coat. Serve cold or at room temperature.

greek salad

This modernized Greek salad combines romaine lettuce and peppery arugula in a light dressing

Serves 6-8 ❋ *Prep time: 15 minutes* ❋ *Cooking time: None*

INGREDIENTS

- **2 heads** romaine lettuce, washed and torn into bite-sized pieces
- **2 bunches** arugula, washed, torn into bite-sized pieces
- **1 ¼ cups** thinly sliced red onion
- **1 ¾ cups** crumbled feta cheese
- **16** cherry tomatoes, cut in half
- **16** pitted whole ripe olives

DRESSING

- **¾ cup** extra-virgin olive oil
- **6 tablespoons** lemon juice
- **2 teaspoons** dried oregano
- **½ teaspoon** dried parsley or 1 ½ teaspoons chopped fresh parsley

salt and black pepper to taste

1. In a small bowl, **WHISK** together olive oil, lemon juice, oregano, parsley. Add salt and pepper to taste. Set aside.

2. In a large bowl, **MIX** together the lettuce, arugula, red onion, feta cheese, tomatoes, and olives.

3. **GENTLY POUR** dressing over lettuce mixture and **TOSS.** Serve immediately.

WHAT IS IT? WHERE DO I FIND IT?

ARUGULA is a tangy, mustardy salad green that adds a nice bit of spice when combined with other greens.

❋ ❋ ❋

FETA CHEESE is essential to Greek salad. Feta has a slightly salty tang. It is sold in bricks as well as crumbled and is available in the deli or dairy section at most supermarkets.

garlic roasted potato salad

The perfect side dish to a barbeque or sandwich

Serves 6-8 ✳ *Prep time: 25 minutes* ✳ *Cooking time: 35 minutes*

INGREDIENTS

- **3 pounds** red potatoes, cut into 1-inch cubes
- **3 tablespoons** olive oil
- **1½ tablespoons** Dijon mustard
- **1 teaspoon** mustard powder
- **1 teaspoon** dried coriander
- **8 garlic cloves**, peeled and cut in half
- **1 tablespoon** dried parsley or ¼ cup fresh flat-leaf parsley, chopped
- **1 tablespoon** dried basil or ¼ cup fresh basil, chopped
- **⅔ cup** plain low-fat yogurt
- **¼ cup** green onions (white and green parts) thinly sliced
- **1¼ teaspoons** salt
- **1 teaspoon** black pepper

1. **PREHEAT** oven to 400°F.

2. **COMBINE** first six ingredients in a large mixing bowl. Place mixture in a shallow roasting pan and bake for 30 to 35 minutes, or until potatoes are tender, stirring every five minutes. Remove from oven and let cool to room temperature.

3. **COMBINE** parsley, basil, yogurt, green onions, salt, and pepper in a large bowl. Add potato mixture and stir gently just to combine. Serve at room temperature.

✳ NOW WHAT ?! ✳

How do I tell the difference between flat-leaf parsley and cilantro?
Cilantro, also referred to as fresh coriander, is a tangy green herb that resembles flat-leaf parsley or Italian parsley. Hence the problem. The best way to tell them apart is to take a tiny taste. Cilantro is much stronger in taste than flat parsley—with hints of pepper and lemon.

classic green salad with vinaigrette

Serves 6 ✳ *Prep time: 10 minutes* ✳ *Cooking time: none*

INGREDIENTS

- **1** shallot, minced
- **1 tablespoon** Dijon mustard
- **½ cup** balsamic vinegar or red wine vinegar
- **½ teaspoon** salt
- **1 teaspoon** black pepper
- **1 tablespoon** lime juice
- **1 cup and 2 tablespoons** olive oil

SALAD

- **8 cups** torn salad greens

Garnish (optional):

- **1 cup** chopped hazelnuts

1. In a small jar with a lid, **COMBINE** all vinaigrette ingredients. Shake well to mix. Vinaigrette yields 1 ½ cups.

2. WASH salad greens by swishing them in a large bowl of cold water. Drain in a colander, and pat the leaves dry with paper towels. Better yet, use a salad spinner. Place the greens in the spinner's inner bowl and rinse them under cold running water. Place the inner bowl into the outer bowl, cover, and spin dry.

3. TRANSFER salad greens into a serving bowl. Shake vinaigrette to remix, then pour it over the greens. Toss to mix. Garnish with hazelnuts and serve immediately.

✳ **NOW WHAT ?!** ✳

Q How much vinaigrette should I use?

As much or as little as you want. If in doubt, use 1/8 cup (2 tablespoons) per serving.

caesar salad

An eggless version of a classic salad that is fabulous

Serves 6-8 ✳ *Prep time: 10-15 minutes* ✳ *Cooking time: 18 minutes*

INGREDIENTS

CROUTONS

¾ **teaspoon** garlic powder

½ **teaspoon** black pepper

1 **cup** grated Parmesan cheese

1 **baguette** (long loaf of French or Italian bread)

olive oil for brushing (approximately ⅓ cup)

for the croutons

1. PREHEAT oven to 400°F.

2. In a small bowl, **MIX** together the garlic powder, black pepper, and Parmesan cheese.

3. SLICE the baguette on the diagonal into ½-inch rounds (you'll get about 20 to 25 slices, depending on the size of the bread).

4. PLACE bread slices on a large baking sheet. Brush each slice with olive oil using a pastry brush or the back of a spoon. Sprinkle with the cheese mixture.

5. BAKE bread slices for 15-18 minutes, or until they are brown and slightly crisp. Set aside to cool to room temperature. While croutons are cooling, prepare the dressing.

for the dressing

1. PLACE the lemon juice, garlic, and anchovy paste in a blender or the bowl of a food processor fitted with a steel blade. (Machine blending ensures a smooth consistency.) Blend or pulse until the mixture is combined.

2. ADD mustards. Blend or pulse to combine.

3. While motor is running, gradually **ADD** Parmesan cheese, oil, salt, and pepper. Blend or pulse until mixture is smooth.

for the salad

1. CUT off the base of the romaine lettuce and discard the tough outer leaves. Romaine can be very sandy—rinse whole leaves thoroughly under cool running water or in a pot of cool water. Pat dry with paper towels or use a salad spinner. Cut or tear the lettuce into bite-sized pieces.

2. Place the lettuce leaves in a large serving bowl. Drizzle the Caesar Salad Dressing over the lettuce and **TOSS** gently. Garnish with the cooled Parmesan croutons. Serve immediately.

CAESAR DRESSING

½ **cup** cold lemon juice

5 **cloves** garlic, peeled

1 ½-2 **teaspoons** anchovy paste

1 ¼ **teaspoons** Dijon mustard

¾ **teaspoon** dry mustard

6 **tablespoons** Parmesan cheese, grated

1 **cup plus 2 tablespoons** canola oil

¼ **teaspoon** salt

1 **teaspoon** pepper

SALAD

2 **heads** of romaine lettuce

WHAT IS IT AND WHERE DO I FIND IT?

ANCHOVY PASTE You can use canned or jarred anchovies for the dressing, but the tubes of paste, which have vinegar and spices mixed in, are more convenient for cooking. Look for the paste in grocery stores (near the canned anchovies) or in specialty food markets. Store opened tubes in the fridge.

* * *

DRY MUSTARD is powdered mustard seeds. It's available in the spice section of any supermarket.

wild rice salad

Orange juice and dried cherries complement the nutty flavor of wild rice

Serves 4–6 ✳ *Prep time: 15 minutes* ✳ *Cooking time: 40 minutes*

INGREDIENTS

- 1 **cup** uncooked wild rice
- 1 ½ **cups** low-sodium chicken broth
- 1 ½ **cups** water
- 1 **cup** pine nuts (see next page) or slivered almonds
- 1 **cup** dried cherries (see next page) or dried cranberries or raisins
- ½ **cup** chopped dried apricots
- ¼ **cup** minced shallots
- ¼ **cup** canola oil
- ⅓ **cup** orange juice
- 1 **tablespoon** balsamic vinegar
- ½ **teaspoon** dried thyme
- ½ **teaspoon** salt

1. RINSE wild rice in a strainer under cold water. (You have to rinse it because it's gathered directly from marsh grasses and may contain dirt or twigs.)

2. In a large saucepan, combine rice, broth, and water. Bring to a **BOIL** over high heat so you see nickle-sized bubbles at the surface.

3. Once it's reached boiling point, immediately **REDUCE** heat to low and **SIMMER** (a few pearl-sized bubbles will form every minute) uncovered for 40 minutes. Do not stir.

4. DRAIN rice in a colander or strainer. (Take a taste, it should be a bit crunchy.)

5. In a large bowl, **COMBINE** rice with remaining ingredients. Mix well and let stand at room temperature for up to four hours or until ready to serve.

WHAT IS IT AND WHERE DO I FIND IT?

PINE NUTS (also called pignoli nuts) are edible seeds that grow in the cones of various pine trees. Although expensive, they add wonderful flavor and crunch. Pine nuts are about the size of TicTacs, and are usually sold in little containers where nuts are found at grocery, health food, and gourmet food stores. Store them in the refrigerator.

* * *

DRIED CHERRIES can be found in the produce section of most supermarkets. If you can't find them or don't like cherries, try dried cranberries. Dried fruit keeps well if stored in a plastic bag in the cupboard.

For those who love their food full of flavor and texture, take a bite of Wild Rice Salad.

warm lentil salad

Lentils aren't just for soup—try them in this salad and experience their hearty flavor

Serves 4-6   ✳   *Prep time: 15 minutes*   ✳   *Cooking time: 30 minutes*

INGREDIENTS

4 ½   **cups** water

1 ¼   **cups** dried lentils (picked over, see note on next page)

¼   **cup** olive oil

2   **tablespoons** red wine vinegar

2   **tablespoons** orange juice

1   **teaspoon** dried oregano

3   **cloves** garlic, minced

½   **teaspoon** dried chervil or parsley

¼   **teaspoon** salt

½   **teaspoon** black pepper

4   **ounces** feta cheese, crumbled

3   **cups** torn Bibb or romaine lettuce, rinsed and dried

1. In a saucepan, **COMBINE** water and lentils over medium heat and bring to a **BOIL** (so you see nickle-sized bubbles).

2. As soon as the water bubbles, **COVER** the saucepan and reduce heat to low. **SIMMER** (with pearl-sized bubbles coming to the surface every minute or so) until lentils are chewable but not mushy—about 25 to 30 minutes. **DRAIN** lentils in a colander and set aside.

3. In a medium-sized bowl **COMBINE** oil, vinegar, orange juice, oregano, garlic, chervil, salt, and pepper.

4. **ADD** lentils, feta cheese, and lettuce and toss gently.

5. **SERVE** warm or at room temperature with toast points or pita bread.

WHAT IS IT? WHERE DO I FIND IT?

LENTILS are slightly smaller and flatter than peas. There are several varieties which are easily distinguished from one another because they are naturally different colors. The kind most often found in supermarkets are green or brown. French lentils are greenish and really tiny—about the size of pinheads. Indian lentils are bright orange. Lentils are sold in bags in supermarkets. Health food stores and Middle Eastern or Indian groceries sell them bagged or in bulk. Unlike dried beans, they don't need to be soaked before cooking. You should sort through them, though, and discard any stems or bits of gravel you may find, then rinse them in a colander before using them in a recipe.

FIRST PERSON DISASTER

Bubbles, Toil, and Trouble

It was my first time cooking lentils. I liked the fact that you didn't have to soak them like other dried beans. So I popped them in the pot with the water, covered the pot, and turned the stove to low to simmer them. "Low" is clearly a word open for discussion in cooking. I turned my stove to its lowest setting. Every now and then I checked the pot. The lentils were just lying there in the water. After 25 minutes, I tasted the lentils. They were as hard as pebbles. I called my mom. What went wrong? She asked if I had seen any bubbles coming to the surface while the lentils were cooking. Well, no, not really. "Then you weren't cooking them, you were just warming them." Swell. She suggested I crank up the stove to a higher setting and let the lentils simmer. After 10 minutes, I could taste the difference. I had cooked lentils at last!

Jesse R., Yonkers, New York

new wave spinach salad

Couldn't be easier. Instead of the traditional spinach salad with bacon, this one features fruit and lemon juice

Serves 6 ✳ *Prep time: 10-15 minutes* ✳ *Cooking time: none*

INGREDIENTS

- ¼ **cup** lemon juice
- 8 **tablespoons** canola oil
- 2 **tablespoons** honey
- 1 **teaspoon** Dijon mustard
- 2 **cloves** garlic, peeled and minced
- ½ **teaspoon** salt
- 1 **teaspoon** black pepper

SALAD

- 3 **cups** torn spinach leaves, washed and dried
- 3 **cups** torn red leaf lettuce, washed and dried
- 2 ripe kiwi fruit, peeled and thinly sliced
- 1 **can** (11 ounces) Mandarin oranges, drained
- ½ **cup** dried cranberries
- 1 **cup** red onion, thinly sliced
- 6 **ounces** soft goat cheese, cut into six ½ - inch-thick rounds

1. In a small bowl, **WHISK** together lemon juice, oil, honey, mustard, garlic, salt and pepper. Set aside.

2. COMBINE spinach and lettuce in a large bowl.

3. POUR dressing over greens and toss to coat.

4. DIVIDE greens among 6 plates and garnish each with kiwi, cranberries, red onion, and a round of goat cheese. Serve with a crusty slice of bread.

WHAT IS IT? WHERE DO I FIND IT?

DRIED CRANBERRIES They are sold in small bags and can be found in the produce section of most supermarkets, health food and gourmet stores. If you can't find them, try dried cherries. As a last resort, you can use raisins.

* * *

KIWI FRUIT Once an exotic rarity imported from New Zealand, it's now grown in the U.S. and available all year round in most supermarket produce sections. Although the skin is a little hard to remove, do your best since it's too fuzzy to eat. Use a good sharp knife.

Q How do I tell if a kiwi is ripe?

A ripe kiwi will give slightly when you touch it and will keep at room temperature for 2 to 3 days.

• • •

Q I have a really hard time cutting goat cheese into rounds. Any ideas ?

Yes, several. For starters the cheese will slice more easily if you cut it while it's cold—then use it at room temperature. Cut it with a sharp knife, or try dental floss to cut through it.

New Wave Spinach Salad makes a gorgeous main course for an elegant lunch.

asparagus salad with parmesan

If it's spring, it must be asparagus season—they're perfect in salads

Serves 6 ✳ *Prep time: 10 minutes* ✳ *Cooking time: 1 minute*

INGREDIENTS

2 pounds pencil-thin asparagus, ends trimmed (see note)

DRESSING

½ **cup** olive oil

4 tablespoons champagne vinegar or white wine vinegar

1 ½ **tablespoons** Dijon mustard

1 tablespoon minced shallots

½ **teaspoon** black pepper

¼ **teaspoon** salt

½ **cup** grated Parmesan cheese (see note)

1. Bring a large pot of water to a **BOIL** (you'll see nickle-sized bubbles roiling up.) Add the asparagus and reduce the heat to a **SIMMER** (cook gently in water that's bubbling slightly) for 1 minute, or until asparagus is just tender. Drain immediately over a colander and rinse under cold water to stop the cooking process.

2. Pat asparagus dry with paper towels and place in a serving bowl.

3. In a small bowl **WHISK** together the dressing ingredients. Gently pour over asparagus and toss so there's enough dressing to coat.

3. **SPRINKLE** with Parmesan cheese and serve.

🔘 How do I trim asparagus?

Take hold of an asparagus stalk with both hands—one at the root end and one at the tip. Bend until it snaps and discard the bottom. If this strikes you as too wasteful (sometimes you'll lose half the stalk), there's nothing wrong with just cutting off the tough bottom end with a knife. Pencil-thin asparagus doesn't require peeling, but if they're fatter than your little finger, peel the bottoms as you would a carrot.

• • •

🔘 I always overcook my asparagus. How do I avoid that?

Ideally, asparagus should be cooked standing up in water with the tender tips above water level. Use kitchen string to tie the stalks together so they'll stand up easily. If the asparagus is thin, it won't take more than a minute or two to cook. If it is thick, cook it a bit longer, but check it frequently to avoid overcooking.

• • •

🔘 I'd like to use fresh Parmesan cheese. Is it hard to grate?

Fresh Parmesan cheese tastes so much better than the pre-packaged grated kind that you won't believe it until you try it. The good news is that a chunk of fresh Parmesan cheese will last a month or two in the refrigerator. To shave it, use a vegetable (or carrot) peeler. Or take out your cheese grater and use the large blade on the side.

vegetable couscous salad

Couscous, a lovely cross between rice and barley, lends texture and flavor to any salad

Serves 6 ✸ *Prep time: 15 minutes* ✸ *Cooking time: 6 minutes*

INGREDIENTS

- 1 ½ **cups** low-sodium chicken broth
- 1 **cup** uncooked couscous
- ⅓ **pound** fresh asparagus, trimmed (see page 67) and cut into 1-inch pieces
- ⅓ **cup** chopped red bell pepper
- ⅓ **cup** chopped yellow bell pepper
- ⅔ **cup** cherry tomatoes, halved
- 3 scallions (both white and green parts), thinly sliced
- ¼ **cup** orange juice
- 2 **tablespoons** balsamic vinegar
- 2 **teaspoons** olive oil
- 1 ½ **teaspoons** dried oregano
- 1 ½ **teaspoons** black pepper
- 1 **teaspoon** ground cumin
- ¼ **teaspoon** salt
- 6 **cups** salad greens, rinsed

1. In a medium saucepan, bring broth to a **BOIL** (so you see nickle-sized bubbles.) Remove saucepan from heat and stir in couscous.

2. **COVER** the saucepan and let stand for 5 minutes. Take a look, the couscous should be fully cooked. Fluff it with a fork and transfer to a large bowl. Set aside.

3. In another medium saucepan, bring one quart of water to a full boil (rolling nickle-sized bubbles). **ADD** the asparagus to boiling water and cook for 1 minute. Drain in a colander and rinse immediately under cold water to stop the cooking process. Pat dry with paper towels.

4. In a large bowl, **COMBINE** couscous, asparagus, red and yellow bell peppers, tomatoes, and scallions, tossing gently.

5. In a small bowl, **WHISK** together orange juice, balsamic vinegar, olive oil, oregano, black pepper, cumin, and salt. Pour over couscous mixture; toss gently.

6. **COVER** and chill for up to 24 hours. Remove from refrigerator at least 30 minutes before serving.

Vegetable couscous salad makes an easy light lunch.

7. When ready to serve, **ARRANGE** a bed of salad greens on plates and place a generous serving of the couscous salad (about 1 cup) in the center of each plate.

WHAT IS IT? WHERE DO I FIND IT?

COUSCOUS Think of couscous as the rice of North Africa. It's a tiny grain of semolina—the same grain that pasta flour is made from. Most U.S. supermarkets now carry an instant packaged version in the ethnic or health food aisle.

4 Vegetables

Side dishes can often make the meal. Choose from Sesame Asparagus (top), Lemon-Dilled Carrots (middle), and Green Bean Medley (bottom).

roasted zucchini

An easy and delicious way to enjoy this plentiful summer vegetable— use fresh herbs if possible

Serves 4-6 ✳ *Prep time: 15 minutes* ✳ *Cooking time: 6 minutes*

INGREDIENTS

Vegetable oil cooking spray

- **4 medium** zucchini
- ¼ **cup** melted butter
- ¼ **cup** olive oil
- **1 tablespoon** dried basil or ½ cup fresh basil, minced
- **1 tablespoon** dried thyme or ½ cup fresh thyme, minced
- **2 tablespoons** black pepper
- ⅔ **cup** grated Parmesan cheese

1. **PREHEAT** the oven to 400°F.

2. **SPRAY** a large baking sheet with vegetable oil cooking spray.

3. **SCRUB** the zucchini, trim the ends, and slice them into 1-inch-thick rounds.

4. **COMBINE** the melted butter and olive oil in a small bowl and set it aside.

5. **PLACE** the zucchini rounds on the baking sheet. Using a pastry brush (see page 7), brush the rounds lightly with the butter and oil mixture.

6. **SPRINKLE** herbs and pepper over the rounds; then sprinkle the grated Parmesan cheese.

7. **BAKE** the zucchini for 5 to 6 minutes, or until they are golden brown.

Ⓠ How do I grate fresh Parmesan cheese?

This aged Italian cheese is sold in wedges and can be found in most supermarket cheese sections. To grate it, simply use the box grater as you would for any other cheese. (The large holes are easiest.) For a speedier clean-up, spray the grater with vegetable oil before grating. You can also use a food processor fitted with a grating disc to speed up your preparation.

● ● ●

Ⓠ Why do you use both butter and oil to coat the zucchini ?

They both add their own distinctive flavors to the zucchini. Also, the oil has a higher burning point than the butter, and will allow the zucchini to cook longer without browning too soon.

green bean medley

A colorful salad full of delicious flavor and texture

Serves 4-6 ✳ *Prep time: 15 minutes* ✳ *Cooking time: 10 minutes*

INGREDIENTS

- 1 ¼ **pounds** fresh green beans, stem ends trimmed
- 2 **tablespoons** canola or vegetable oil
- 1 red bell pepper, cored, seeded, and diced
- 1 yellow bell pepper, cored, seeded, and diced
- ⅓ **cup** chopped red onion
- 2 **teaspoons** minced garlic
- 1 **teaspoon** dried basil
- ½ **teaspoon** dried thyme
- ½ **teaspoon** black pepper
- ¾ **cup** grated Parmesan cheese

1. **MICROWAVE** the green beans in a covered microwaveable dish with 1 tablespoon of water for 2 to 3 minutes or until crisp, but tender. Drain them in a colander, then rinse with very cold water to stop the cooking process; drain again. Cut beans into 2-inch pieces and set aside.

2. **HEAT** the oil in a large, heavy skillet over medium heat for 30 seconds. **ADD** the bell peppers, onion, and garlic and cook for 2 to 3 minutes, or until they are slightly soft.

3. **ADD** the basil, thyme, and pepper and cook for 1 minute.

4. **ADD** the cooled green beans and cook for about 2 minutes, until heated through, stirring to combine.

5. **REMOVE** the vegetables from the heat and stir in ½ cup of the Parmesan cheese.

6. **TRANSFER** the vegetables to a serving bowl and sprinkle with remaining cheese. Serve immediately.

Green Bean Medley is a feast for both the eye and the palate.

spinach with white beans

Equally delicious served hot, cold, or at room temperature. Ideal with a grilled fish fillet or chicken breast

Serves 4-6 ✳ *Prep time: 10 minutes* ✳ *Cooking time: 15-20 minutes*

INGREDIENTS

2-3 tablespoons canola oil

6 cloves garlic, minced

2 large leeks (white and pale-green parts), washed, dried, and sliced thin, or 1 cup chopped onion

2 cans (14½ ounces each) diced tomatoes, with juice

2 boxes (10 ounces each) frozen cut leaf spinach, thawed and squeezed dry (see page 23)

2 cans (15½ ounces each) small white beans, rinsed and drained

1 teaspoon dried thyme

½ teaspoon dried basil

½ teaspoon dried oregano

Salt and black pepper to taste

1 tablespoon lemon juice

1. HEAT the oil in a large non-stick skillet over medium heat for 30 seconds.

2. ADD the garlic and leeks or onions and **sauté** (cook over medium heat, stirring occasionally so they don't burn) for 3-4 minutes.

3. STIR in the tomatoes and their juices and simmer for 5-6 minutes.

4. ADD the spinach to the mixture and stir to combine. Continue cooking until the vegetables are heated through, about 2-3 minutes.

5. STIR in the beans, thyme, basil, and oregano, and cook the mixture for 5-7 minutes more. Add salt and pepper to taste and sprinkle with the lemon juice.

6. TRANSFER the vegetables to a serving bowl and serve.

WHAT IS IT AND WHERE DO I FIND IT?

LEEKS are related to onions and have a sweet, mild, oniony flavor that goes well in soups, potato dishes, and stews. (They look a bit like large scallions.) You want young tender leeks that are about one inch in diameter and about 9 to 12 inches long. The stalks of leeks can be full of dirt and must be thoroughly washed. To clean them, trim off the rough ends of the dark green leaves and discard. Make a slit down the center of the leek and pull it apart. Wash each half thoroughly under cold water, bending them back to rinse away every bit of grit hidden between the layers. Pat them dry with paper towels.

sesame asparagus

When asparagus is not available, you can substitute broccoli—either one is a wonderful accompaniment to grilled entrées, from shrimp to steak

Serves 6 ✳ *Prep time: 10-15 minutes* ✳ *Cooking time: 8-10 minutes*

INGREDIENTS

2 pounds fresh asparagus, ends trimmed (see page 67) and stalks cut into thirds

2 tablespoons canola oil

4 teaspoons garlic, minced

2-4 tablespoons sesame oil

1 ½ tablespoons lemon juice

2 teaspoons low-sodium soy sauce

Salt and pepper to taste

3 tablespoons sesame seeds

1. BRING a medium-sized pot of water to a boil over high heat (you'll see nickle-sized bubbles). Drop in the asparagus, reduce the heat to medium, and cook for about 1 minute, until they are crisp, but tender.

2. DRAIN the asparagus in a colander and immediately rinse under cold water to stop the cooking process. Drain again and set aside.

3. HEAT the canola oil in a large non-stick skillet over medium-high heat for 1 minute.

4. ADD the garlic and cook, stirring, for about 30 seconds. (Be careful not to let the garlic burn.)

5. ADD the asparagus and 2 tablespoons of sesame oil to the skillet, stirring constantly to coat the asparagus with oil. (Add additional sesame oil if needed.) Cook the asparagus, tossing, for 1 to 2 more minutes.

6. POUR the lemon juice and soy sauce over the asparagus and stir well. Add salt and pepper to taste. Sprinkle sesame seeds over the asparagus and toss well.

7. TRANSFER the asparagus to a serving dish and serve.

Sesame seeds and a bit of soy sauce and lemon juice turn ordinary asparagus into an exciting side dish.

zucchini squares

Serve these delicious creations as a side dish or a main course for a brunch or lunch

Serves 6 as a side dish; 4 main-course servings ✳ *Prep time: 25 minutes*
✳ *Cooking time: 20-25 minutes*

INGREDIENTS

Vegetable oil cooking spray

- **3 pounds** zucchini, scrubbed clean, trimmed, and grated (see note on page 47)
- **2 tablespoons** butter
- **2 tablespoons** canola or vegetable oil
- **5 cloves** garlic, chopped
- **1 cup** chopped scallions, white and green parts
- **1 whole egg**, lightly beaten
- **2 egg** whites, lightly beaten
- **½ cup** grated Parmesan cheese
- **⅓ cup** bread crumbs
- **1 ½ tablespoons** dried basil or 1 ¼ cup fresh basil, rinsed and chopped

Salt and pepper to taste

1. PREHEAT the oven to 350°F.

2. COAT an 8-inch square baking pan with vegetable oil cooking spray and set aside.

3. SPREAD the grated zucchini on paper towels or clean dish towels, rolling them up jelly-roll style to absorb any excess water. Place the zucchini in a large bowl and set it aside.

4. HEAT the butter and oil in a large skillet over medium-high heat until butter is melted (about 30 seconds).

5. ADD the garlic and scallions to the skillet and cook over medium heat, stirring frequently, until lightly browned, about 2 to 3 minutes.

6. ADD the scallion mixture to the zucchini, stirring to combine. Add the whole egg, egg whites, Parmesan cheese, bread crumbs, basil, and salt and pepper to taste. Stir to combine.

7. TRANSFER the zucchini mixture to the baking dish, and bake 20 to 25 minutes until firm in the center and light brown on top. To test that it's firm in the center, jiggle the pan; if the the center still quivers, bake the zucchini for another 2 to 3 minutes.

8. CUT the zucchini into squares and serve immediately.

"Runny" late

My guests were coming for brunch at 11:30 and I was running late. I had grated the zucchini for a zucchini quiche and had them in the paper towels to soak up all that liquid. I had put out a wonderful bread I had bought at the farmer's market and a salad. Just as I was setting the table, the guests rang the bell. I poured them each a glass of wine and headed back to the kitchen to throw the ingredients for the quiche together—another 10 minutes gone. As I poured the zucchini mixture into the baking dish, I had the bright idea of turning up the heat to speed the baking along. So instead of baking at 350°F for 40 minutes, I turned up the oven to 450°F and baked it for 20 minutes. The result? Burnt on top, dried-out at the edges, and runny in the middle. By trying to save 20 minutes, I ruined my brunch. At least the salad and bread were edible.

Marjorie P., Riverhead, Connecticut

acorn squash with citrus herb sauce

Serve alongside any pork or poultry dish

Serves 6 ✳ *Prep time: 10 minutes* ✳ *Cooking time: 1 hour in oven; 20 minutes in microwave*

INGREDIENTS

3 medium acorn squash, halved and seeded

salt and black pepper to taste

6 teaspoons butter

4 teaspoons dark brown sugar, packed

½ cup orange juice

1 tablespoon orange zest (see note)

1 tablespoon lemon zest (see note)

1 teaspoon dried thyme

1 teaspoon dried oregano

1 teaspoon ground cinnamon

1. PREHEAT the oven to 350°F.

2. SEASON the squash with salt and pepper to taste. Place the squash halves in a baking pan, cut side down, and add 1 inch of water to the pan.

3. BAKE the squash, uncovered, 50 to 60 minutes or until the fleshy underside is tender when pierced with a fork. Remove the squash halves from the oven, and invert them so that the flesh side is up. Set them aside.

4. COMBINE the butter, brown sugar, orange juice, orange zest, lemon zest, thyme, and oregano in a small saucepan. Cook the sauce over medium-low heat for 5 minutes, stirring, until it has the consistency of a vinaigrette salad dressing.

5. SPOON the sauce evenly into the scooped-out squash halves, stir slightly to blend it. Return the squash to the oven and bake 5 to 10 minutes.

6. REMOVE the squash halves from the oven. Sprinkle with cinnamon and serve immediately.

WHAT IS IT? WHERE DO I FIND IT?

ACORN SQUASH is about the size of a large grapefruit. It has thick dark-green skin, with deep grooves running up and down its sides. Inside, the flesh is yellow-orange (it's loaded with vitamin A). It's available in produce sections most frequently during fall and winter.

* * *

LEMON AND ORANGE ZEST are not sold in stores; you have to make zest yourself. How? Get a fresh orange or lemon, a cheese grater, and a plate. Wash the fruit. Put the plate under the grater and rub the fruit over the side that has the smallest holes. You should see little powdery flecks on the plate—that's the zest. (Avoid grating the white pith under the bright-colored skin; it's not at all tasty.)

lemon-dilled carrots

Lemon and dill add a sophisticated touch to a tried-and-true favorite

Serves 6-8 ✳ *Prep time: 10 minutes* ✳ *Cooking time: 10 minutes*

INGREDIENTS

- **10 medium-sized** carrots, peeled and sliced on the diagonal
- **1½ teaspoons** cornstarch
- **1 tablespoon** plus **1 teaspoon** lemon juice
- **½ cup** water
- **1¼ teaspoons** margarine
- **1 teaspoon** dried dill, or 2 teaspoons chopped fresh dill
- **½ teaspoon** grated lemon zest (see page 83)
- **¼ teaspoon** salt
- **1 teaspoon** black pepper
- **2 teaspoons** honey
- **Garnish** (optional): fresh dill sprigs

1. STEAM the sliced carrots using a vegetable steamer for 2 minutes, or until they are crisp but tender (see note using a steamer). Or place the carrots in a microwaveable dish and microwave on high for 3 to 4 minutes. Drain the carrots in a colander (but don't run cold water over carrots after steaming). Set the colander aside and cover it with a tent made of aluminum foil to keep carrots warm.

2. COMBINE the cornstarch, lemon juice and water in a small saucepan, stirring until they are blended. Then stir in the water.

3. PLACE the pan over medium heat and cook, stirring constantly, until the mixture thickens. It should look like very thin pancake batter.

4. ADD the margarine, dill, lemon zest, salt, pepper, and honey; cook, stirring the sauce constantly, until the margarine is melted.

5. TRANSFER the carrots to a serving dish and pour the sauce over them, tossing to combine. Garnish if desired.

Lemon and dill turn everyday
carrots into a gourmet side dish.

✳ NOW WHAT?! ✳

Q I've never used a vegetable steamer before, how does it work?

A steamer is a perforated metal basket that stands above the water
level in a saucepan (see page 3 for illustration). Place the steamer in a
pot with a lid. (The lid should fit snugly so steam won't escape; this
would defeat your purpose.) Pour water in the pot until just below the
bottom of the steamer. Place the food in the steamer, cover the pot,
and cook for as long as the recipe stipulates. When done, use an oven
mitt and remove the lid slowly.

roasted red potatoes

The perfect accompaniment to so many entrées—
best of all, they are so easy to prepare

Serves 8 ✳ *Prep time: 10 minutes* ✳ *Cooking time: 35-40 minutes*

INGREDIENTS

- **3 pounds** small red-skinned potatoes, cut into 1½ -inch pieces
- **2 tablespoons** chopped garlic
- **1½ tablespoons** dried rosemary, crumbled, or 3 tablespoons fresh rosemary, minced
- **1 teaspoon** salt
- **1 teaspoon** black pepper
- **⅓ cup** olive oil

1. PREHEAT oven to 400°F.

2. COMBINE all the ingredients in a large bowl. Toss so that potatoes are coated on all sides with the oil and seasonings.

3. TRANSFER potatoes to a large baking dish or roasting pan, and bake for 35 to 40 minutes or until potatoes are tender inside and browned and crisp outside. Stir them every 15 minutes so the potatoes cook evenly.

4. SERVE immediately.

garlic mashed potatoes

A new spin on an old-time standard

Serves 6-8 ✳ *Prep time: 15 minutes* ✳ *Roasting time for garlic: 45 minutes*
✳ *Cooking time for potatoes: 15–20 minutes*

INGREDIENTS

1	**large** whole head of garlic
1 ½	**tablespoons** olive oil
2	**pounds** Yukon Gold potatoes, peeled and quartered
½	**cup** skim milk
¾	**cup** plain low-fat yogurt
1	**teaspoon** salt
1	**teaspoon** black pepper

1. PREHEAT oven to 375°F.

2. REMOVE papery skin from garlic head, keeping head whole; rub oil over garlic head and wrap in foil. Bake for 45 minutes; cool 10 minutes. Separate the cloves and squeeze to extract the pulp. Discard skins and set garlic aside.

3. PLACE potatoes in a large pot and cover with water. Bring to a boil on medium-high heat and cook 15 to 20 minutes, or until tender when pierced with a fork, drain in a colander and set aside.

4. HEAT milk in a small saucepan over low heat until just warm, or microwave in a microwave dish for 30 seconds.

5. PLACE cooked potatoes in a medium-sized mixing bowl. Pour milk over potatoes and **BEAT** at medium speed using an electric mixer until potatoes are smooth. Beat in yogurt, salt, and pepper; mix until smooth. Add garlic pulp and stir with a spoon to combine. Season with more salt and pepper to suit your taste.

6. SERVE immediately.

sweet potato gratin

A gratin is a dish topped with cheese or bread crumbs—
here it's Parmesan cheese and chives

Serves 6-8 ✴ *Prep time: 20 minutes* ✴ *Cooking time: 1 hour, 15 minutes*

INGREDIENTS

Vegetable oil cooking spray

- ¾ **cup** light cream
- ¾ **cup** sherry or white wine
- 2 **teaspoons** minced shallots
- ½ **teaspoon** salt
- 1 **teaspoon** ground white pepper (see next page)
- ½ **teaspoon** ground nutmeg
- 1 ½ **pounds** white potatoes
- 1 ½ **pounds** sweet potatoes
- 2 **teaspoons** dried chives, or ¼ **cup** chopped fresh chives
- 1 **cup** grated Parmesan cheese

1. **PREHEAT** oven to 350°F.

2. **COAT** a 9-inch square baking pan with cooking spray.

3. **COMBINE** cream, sherry, shallots, salt, white pepper, and nutmeg in a small bowl; set aside.

4. **FILL** two large bowls three-quarters full of cold water. **PEEL** the white potatoes and slice them into ¼-inch rounds. Drop the slices into one of the bowls of water so they will not discolor. Peel and slice the sweet potatoes, placing them in the other bowl.

5. **DRAIN** the potatoes and pat dry. Using about half the slices, **ARRANGE** a single layer of white potatoes on the bottom of the pan; overlap the slices slightly. Drizzle with part of the cream mixture.

6. COVER the layer of white potatoes with a layer of sweet potatoes, overlapping the slices. (Again, use about half the slices.) Drizzle lightly with part of cream mixture. Sprinkle half of the chives and half of the Parmesan cheese over this layer.

7. LAYER the remaining white potatoes on top of the cheese and chives. Drizzle with the cream mixture. Add a layer of the remaining sweet potatoes. Pour the rest of the cream mixture over the potatoes. Sprinkle with the remaining chives and Parmesan cheese.

8. COVER the pan with aluminum foil and bake for 35 minutes. Remove the foil and bake 40 minutes or until the cheese is browned and the potatoes are tender. Serve hot.

WHAT IS IT? WHERE DO I FIND IT?

WHITE PEPPER is made from white, rather than black, peppercorns. Because it is white, it is not visible in white cream sauces or mashed potatoes. You can find it in the spice section of your supermarket.

5 One Pot Meals

Hearty, delicious meals in one dish.
What could be better? Try Penne
with Shrimp and Feta (top), Spinach
Pie (middle), and Shepherd's Pie
(bottom).

black bean chili

Black beans and ground turkey go together beautifully to create a substantially lighter "chili"

Serves 6-8 ✳ *Prep time: 30 minutes* ✳ *Cooking time: 50-60 minutes*

INGREDIENTS

- **1 tablespoon** olive oil
- **1** large yellow onion, chopped
- **6 cloves** garlic, minced
- **1 ¼ pounds** ground turkey
- **6 cups** canned diced tomatoes, with juices
- **2 celery** ribs, washed and cut into 1-inch chunks
- **1 ½ teaspoons** Dijon mustard
- **1 ½ teaspoons** ground cumin
- **2 teaspoons** chili powder
- **4 cans** (15.5 ounces each) black beans, rinsed and drained
- **1 cup** low-sodium chicken broth
- **2 tablespoons** balsamic vinegar

Salt and black pepper to taste

- **⅓ cup** lime juice

Garnish (optional): sour cream, chopped scallions or cilantro, or cheddar or grated Parmesan cheese

1. HEAT the oil in a large stockpot (see page 3) over medium heat for about 20 seconds.

2. ADD the onion and garlic and cook for 2 to 3 minutes, until the onion is translucent.

3. ADD the turkey, tomatoes, celery, mustard, cumin, and chili powder, and cook for about 5 minutes. Break up the turkey with a long wooden spoon and stir mixture occasionally.

4. ADD the beans and reduce the heat to low. Cook uncovered for about 40 to 45 minutes, until the soup thickens. If it thickens after 30 minutes of cooking, add some chicken broth, ¼ cup at a time.

5. ADD the vinegar, salt, and pepper and cook for 5 minutes. Stir in the lime juice.

6. SERVE garnished with sour cream, grated cheddar or Parmesan cheese, chopped scallions, or cilantro if desired.

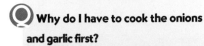

Why do I have to cook the onions and garlic first?

The process of sautéeing onions and garlic before adding them to a soup or stew enhances the finished dish by releasing more of their flavor.

FIRST PERSON DISASTER

Burned Once, Burned Twice

It was Superbowl Sunday and I always make chili for my friends. I put it all together and let it simmer on the stove and went to watch the game. What can I say? My team was ahead by one field goal and I was screaming so loudly I couldn't hear the kitchen timer. When I finally went back to the kitchen to get more beer, I realized that the chili had been cooking for over an hour without being stirred. And what was that horrible smell? I checked the pot and stirred it, scraping the bottom, and discovered the chili had burned and stuck to the bottom of the pot. No problem, I'll just stir the burnt part in and no one will notice. Wrong! Everyone noticed. Maybe it was the mouthfuls of burnt beans that gave me away. My girlfriend said I should not have stirred the already burnt part into the chili and just poured the chili into another pot, the burnt stuff would have stayed behind. Well, at least my team won. Next year it's pizza.

Michael T., Sunapee, New Hampshire

spinach pie

All the taste of spanakopita, but without the hassle of phyllo dough—flaky pre-made puff pastry does the job

Serves 6-8 ✹ *Prep time: 20 minutes* ✹ *Cooking time: 1 hour and 15 minutes*

INGREDIENTS

2½ **tablespoons** olive oil

2½ **cups** chopped Spanish or yellow onions

2 **teaspoons** salt

2 **teaspoons** black pepper

3 **boxes (10 ounces each)** frozen chopped spinach, thawed, squeezed dry (see page 23)

4 **extra-large** whole eggs, lightly beaten

2 **extra-large** egg whites, lightly beaten

2½ **teaspoons** ground nutmeg

2 **teaspoons** dried dill, or 2 tablespoons chopped fresh dill

½ **cup** grated Parmesan cheese

⅔ **pound** feta cheese, crumbled

⅔ **cup** pine nuts (see page 61)

1 **sheet** frozen puff pastry, thawed

1. **PREHEAT** the oven to 375°F.

2. In a skillet, heat the olive oil over medium-high heat for 1 minute. **ADD** the onions and cook for 10 to 12 minutes, stirring frequently, so the onions don't burn. The onions should be translucent and slightly browned.

3. **ADD** the salt and pepper and remove skillet from the heat. Set aside and let cool.

4. **PLACE** the spinach in a large bowl and stir in the cooked onion, then the eggs, egg whites, nutmeg, dill, Parmesan cheese, feta cheese, and pine nuts.

5. **ROLL** out the thawed puff pastry to ⅛-inch thickness and line a 9-inch pie plate (glass or aluminum) with it. Crimp the edges of the pastry along the rim of the pie plate with a fork.

6. **POUR** the spinach mixture into the pie plate and spread it to the edges of the pan.

7. **BAKE** the pie for 50 to 60 minutes until the filling is set.

8. REMOVE the pie from the oven and allow it to cool to room temperature. Cut into wedges and serve.

chicken pot pie

A great way to use up leftover chicken or turkey—sure to warm you up on the coldest winter day

Serves 6 ✳ *Prep time: 30 minutes* ✳ *Cooking time: 55 minutes*

INGREDIENTS

1 ½ **tablespoons** olive oil

2 **large** leeks, white and pale-green parts, rinsed (see page 77) and thinly sliced

2 ¼ **cups** low-sodium chicken stock (canned or homemade, see page 50)

3 **carrots**, peeled and diced

8 **ounces** (about 1 ½ cups) sugar snap peas cut in 1-inch pieces, or green peas

1 ½ **cups** frozen corn kernels, thawed

1 ½ **tablespoons** dried parsley

1 ½ **teaspoons** dried thyme

1 **teaspoon** salt and pepper

2 **tablespoons** cornstarch

2 **cups** cooked chicken or turkey cut into chunks

1 **sheet** frozen puff pastry, thawed

(continued on next page)

1. PREHEAT oven to 475° F.

2. HEAT the oil in a skillet over medium-high heat for 1 minute. **ADD** the leeks and cook for 5 minutes, stirring occasionally. **ADD** 2 cups of stock to the skillet.

3. ADD the carrots, snap peas, corn, parsley, thyme, salt and pepper to the skillet. Cover and simmer over low heat 8 to 10 minutes, or until the vegetables are almost tender. Uncover and cook an additional 2 to 3 minutes.

4. In a small bowl, **STIR** the cornstarch and ¼ cup of the remaining stock together until combined. It should look like a thin paste. Add it to the vegetable mixture and stir for 1 minute, until the liquid begins to thicken slightly.

5. ADD the chicken chunks to the skillet. Stir until the chicken chunks are coated.

6. TRANSFER the chicken mixture to a 2 ½-quart casserole dish. (The dish should have sides 3 inches high.) **PLACE** the thawed puff pastry sheet over the chicken; the pastry should overlap the edges of the dish slightly. **PRESS** firmly around the outside edges to seal it. **TRIM** any excess with a sharp knife and discard it. With a sharp knife or a fork, poke several holes in the pastry.

7. Optional: **WHISK** together the egg white and water and brush the mixture over the top of the pastry. (This is called an egg wash; it gives the pastry a glossy sheen.)

8. BAKE the pie for 25 minutes, or until the crust is lightly browned. Serve.

(continued from previous page)
Optional:
I egg white
I **tablespoon** water

✳ NOW WHAT?! ✳

🔵 **What does cornstarch do?**

Cornstarch is starch that is extracted from corn kernels and reduced to a silky white powder. It acts as a thickener, especially for sauces. You must mix it with a little cool water or other liquid before adding to a mixture, or you will get lumps in your sauce. Cornstarch is available at your supermarket.

• • •

🔵 **I must have cooked the broth too much because it boiled away and now I don't have enough for the recipe, What do I do?**

Open another can of chicken broth and make up the difference.

shepherd's pie

This traditional English pie takes a bit of time—but it's worth it!

Serves 6 ✳ *Prep time: 45 minutes* ✳ *Cooking time: 45 minutes; 25 minutes for the pie, 20 minutes for the potato topping*

INGREDIENTS

FILLING

2 pounds ground lamb or beef

I large yellow onion, chopped

2-3 cloves garlic, minced

2 carrots, diced

I small fennel bulb, diced (see note)

I large parsnip, peeled and diced (see note)

I teaspoon dried rosemary

I teaspoon turmeric

½ teaspoon ground cinnamon

I ½ cups low-sodium canned beef broth

I tablespoon cornstarch

I tablespoon water

Salt and black pepper, to taste

for the filling

1. COOK the lamb in a large skillet over medium heat for 10 to 12 minutes, until it is just done, breaking up the pieces of meat with the back of a wooden spoon. Pour the drippings into an empty can and discard them.

2. ADD the onion, garlic, carrots, fennel, parsnip, rosemary, turmeric, and cinnamon. Stir together and cook 5 minutes.

3. ADD the beef broth to the skillet and cover. Simmer over low heat 12 to 15 minutes (pearl-sized bubbles will form every few seconds). Uncover the skillet and simmer about 2 minutes more, until most of the juices have evaporated.

4. In a small bowl, **MIX** the cornstarch and water and pour the mixture into the skillet, stirring to combine it with the sauce. The sauce should thicken slightly. Season it to taste with the salt and pepper.

5. TRANSFER the mixture to a 2 ½-quart casserole or a baking dish with sides at least 2 inches high.

for the potato topping

1. PREHEAT the oven to 400°F.

2. BOIL the potatoes in a large pot of water for about 20 minutes or until they are just tender.

3. While the potatoes are cooking, **MELT** the butter in a small skillet over medium heat, watching it carefully to see that it doesn't burn. Add the garlic and cook for about 1 minute, until it is just golden.

4. DRAIN the potatoes and transfer them to a large bowl. Add the butter and garlic mixture, yogurt, milk, and Worcestershire sauce.

5. BEAT the potatoes with a hand-held electric mixer until they are smooth and creamy. Season them to taste with salt and pepper.

6. SPOON the potatoes over the top of the meat mixture, spreading them to the edge of the casserole.

7. BAKE the pie 20 to 25 minutes, until the filling is heated through and the potatoes are golden brown. Cut into wedges and serve immediately.

TOPPING

2 pounds white potatoes, peeled and chopped into 2-inch pieces

3 tablespoons butter

3 tablespoons garlic, minced

½ **cup** plain non-fat yogurt

¼ **cup** skim milk

½ **teaspoon** Worcestershire sauce (optional)

Salt and white pepper to taste

✳ NOW WHAT?! ✳

Q **Can I use instant potates instead?** Yes, you'll need to make about 5 cups.

WHAT IS IT? WHERE DO I FIND IT?

FENNEL is a vegetable which looks a bit like celery and is as crunchy, but has a delicate feathery top. It has a spicy flavor that is similar to licorice, but much more subtle. It's available at most supermarkets.

• • •

PARSNIPS are shaped like carrots but are creamy white or tan-colored. They have a tough, fibrous exterior that has to be removed with a vegetable peeler.

spinach lasagna

This is a crowd-pleasing make-ahead meal

Serves 6 ✳ *Prep time: 25 minutes* ✳ *Cooking time: 50 minutes*

INGREDIENTS

- 1 **tablespoon** olive oil
- 2½ **cups** button mushrooms, sliced
- 1 **cup** shredded carrots
- 1 **large** yellow onion, chopped
- 4 **cloves** garlic, minced
- 1 **teaspoon** dried thyme
- 4 **cups** prepared tomato sauce
- 2 **boxes (10 ounces each)** frozen chopped spinach, thawed, drained, and squeezed dry
- 3 **ounces** fat-free cream cheese, softened
- 1½ **cups** low-fat cottage cheese
- 1 **cup** low-fat ricotta cheese
- 2 **teaspoons** lemon juice
- Vegetable oil cooking spray
- 12 oven ready lasagna noodles
- 1 **bag (8 ounces)** shredded part-skim mozzarella cheese
- ¾ **cup** grated Parmesan cheese

1. HEAT the olive oil in a large non-stick skillet over medium-high heat for about 20 seconds, until it is hot.

2. ADD the mushrooms, carrots, onion, and garlic and **COOK** over medium heat, stirring frequently, for 3 minutes. Stir in the thyme. Remove the skillet from the heat and stir in the tomato sauce. Set skillet aside.

3. In a medium-sized bowl, **COMBINE** the spinach, cream cheese, cottage cheese, ricotta and lemon juice. Stir the spinach-cheese mixture well and set it aside.

4. COOK the lasagna noodles according to package directions (or use pre-cooked lasagna noodles). While noodles are cooking, lightly coat a 13 x 9-inch baking dish with vegetable oil cooking spray.

5. PREHEAT the oven to 325°F.

6. ARRANGE 4 of the lasagna noodles in the bottom of the baking dish.

7. SPOON one-third of the spinach-cream mixture over noodles; spoon one-third of the mushroom-tomato mixture over the spinach; spoon one-third of the mozzarella cheese over the tomato mixture; sprinkle ¼ cup Parmesan cheese on top.

8. REPEAT the layers outlined in steps 6 and 7 twice. (Lasagna may be prepared up to this point, covered and refrigerated one day in advance.)

9. BAKE the lasagna uncovered for 50 minutes, until it is heated through. Serve immediately.

❋ NOW WHAT?! ❋

How will I know when the oil is hot enough to cook garlic or onions or shallots?

The surface of the oil will shimmer slightly, but not to the point of smoking. If you are in doubt, put a drop of water or a bit of the vegetable in the oil. If it sizzles, the oil is hot enough.

• • •

How do I clean mushrooms?

Never immerse mushrooms in water since they act like sponges and absorb liquid very quickly. The best way to clean them is to use a mushroom brush, which you can purchase at most grocery stores and any kitchen supply store. Or, you can brush them off with a damp paper towel. If the mushrooms have a lot of debris on them, place them in a colander and rinse them quickly under cold water. Immediately pat them dry with paper towels.

...d noodle bake

...to feed a hungry crowd

...rep time: 30 minutes ✳ *Cooking time: 1 hour (can be prepared 8 hours in advance, refrigerated, and then baked).*

INGREDIENTS

Vegetable oil cooking spray

- **8 ounces** medium egg noodles
- **1½ pounds** lean ground beef
- **1 cup** sliced mushrooms
- **1 cup** chopped onion
- **3 cloves** garlic, minced
- **16 ounces** no-salt canned tomato sauce
- **1** can (14.5 ounces) diced tomatoes, drained
- **1 teaspoon** Italian seasoning (see note)
- **1 teaspoon** black pepper
- **1 teaspoon** salt
- **1** container (**16 ounces**) non-fat cottage cheese
- **1** container (**8 ounces**) fat-free sour cream
- **4 tablespoons** grated Parmesan cheese

(continued on next page)

1. PREHEAT the oven to 350°F. Coat a casserole with vegetable oil cooking spray. Set aside.

2. COOK the noodles according to package directions; drain them and set aside.

3. PLACE the ground beef, mushrooms, onion, and garlic in a large nonstick skillet over medium-high heat. Cook, stirring frequently, for about 6 minutes, until the beef is browned.

4. SCOOP the cooked ingredients onto a plate covered with a double layer of paper towels. Pour the oil from the skillet into an empty can and discard it. Return the cooked ingredients to the skillet.

5. ADD the tomato sauce, tomatoes, Italian seasoning, salt, and pepper; stir to combine. Cook over medium-low heat for about 12 minutes. Remove the sauce from the heat.

6. In a large bowl, **COMBINE** the cottage cheese, sour cream, and Parmesan cheese.

7. ADD the meat mixture to the bowl, together with the noodles and half of the cheese mixture. Stir to combine the ingredients.

8. SPOON the mixture into the casserole dish. (The dish can be prepared up to this point, covered with plastic wrap, and refrigerated for up to 8 hours. When ready to bake, remove the casserole from the refrigerator and let it stand at room temperature for 20 minutes before baking.)

9. BAKE, uncovered, for 25 minutes. Remove the dish from the oven and sprinkle the top with the shredded cheese. Return the dish to the oven for an additional 5 minutes, or until the cheese has melted. Serve.

WHAT IS IT? WHERE DO I FIND IT?

ITALIAN SEASONING can be found in most supermarket spice sections, or you can use a combination of thyme, oregano, basil, and marjoram.

(continued from previous page)

4 ounces shredded low-fat sharp cheddar or Monterey Jack cheese, or a combination

✳ NOW WHAT?! ✳

Can I substitute fresh herbs for dried ones, and vice versa?

Yes, although fresh herbs have brighter flavors than dried herbs. One tablespoon of a chopped fresh herb is the equivalent of one teaspoon of a dried herb. The ratio is 3 fresh herbs to 1 dried herb.

• • •

What should I do if my dried herbs are more than six months old and have lost some of their flavor?

Add a bit more of the dried herb to the recipe to increase the flavor.

deep dish beef burgundy pie

A classic dish that is sure to please

Serves 6 ✳ *Prep time: 45 minutes* ✳ *Cooking time: 45 minutes; 20 minutes for the filling, 25 minutes for the pie*

INGREDIENTS

- **1 tablespoon** flour
- **½ teaspoon each** salt and black pepper
- **2 pounds** boneless beef chuck, cut into 1½-inch pieces
- **1 tablespoon** olive oil
- **3 tablespoons** butter
- **2 onions**, peeled and diced
- **2 teaspoons** minced garlic
- **2 cups** diced carrots
- **2 cups** diced red potatoes
- **1½ tablespoons** Dijon mustard
- **1 cup** red wine
- **1 cup** canned beef broth
- **1 tablespoon** balsamic vinegar
- **2 tablespoons** dried parsley

(continued on next page)

1. COMBINE the flour, salt, and pepper in a large bowl. **ADD** the beef and toss with a fork until the pieces are thoroughly coated with the flour mixture. Set the bowl aside.

2. HEAT the olive oil and 2 tablespoons of the butter in a large skillet over medium heat until the butter melts. Add the onions and garlic and cook for 2 to 3 minutes. Transfer the vegetables from the pan to a plate, using a slotted spoon. Set the plate aside.

3. ADD the beef to the same skillet and cook for 2 to 3 minutes on each side, until the pieces are brown. (The browning may have to be finished in batches.)

4. ADD the cooked onions and garlic, carrots, potatoes, mustard, red wine, broth, vinegar, parsley, thyme, and brown sugar to the skillet and stir to combine. Increase the heat to high and bring the mixture to a boil. Reduce the heat to medium-low, and **SIMMER** (a few pearl-sized bubbles will appear every minute), uncovered, for 1 hour.

5. When the beef is almost done simmering, melt the remaining butter in a medium-sized skillet over low heat.

Add the mushrooms, increase the heat to medium-high, and cook, stirring frequently, for 2 minutes.

6. ADD the mushrooms and peas to the beef mixture. Continue simmering for 3 minutes.

7. PREHEAT the oven to 425°F.

8. POUR the beef mixture into a 2½-quart casserole dish. Place the puff pastry sheet on top. Trim the edges, leaving a 1-inch overhang. **CRIMP** (pinch in a pretty pattern) the pastry to seal the edge of the dish. Place the dish on a baking sheet. **VENT** the pastry by cutting a few slits in the top. (Venting lets steam release slowly from the pie so the filling does not boil over.)

9. BAKE the pie for 25 minutes, or until the pastry is lightly browned. Serve immediately.

(continued from previous page)

- **2 teaspoons** dried thyme
- **2 tablespoons** brown sugar
- **½ pound** fresh mushrooms, sliced
- **1 cup** frozen green peas, thawed
- **1 sheet** frozen puff pastry, thawed and rolled to ¼-inch thickness (see page 95)

❋ **NOW WHAT?!** ❋

🔘 **I don't have any good red wine in the house. Will some other spirits do instead?**

Yes, you can substitute sherry or Madeira—use the same amount the recipe calls for. Otherwise, borrow some good red wine from a neighbor. The wine or spirits you use will impact the flavor of the dish.

chicken and wild rice casserole

Turn chicken into a one-dish wonder with this delicious combination of wild rice and mushrooms

Serves 6 ✳ *Prep time: 25 minutes (not including cooking time for wild rice)* ✳ *Cooking time: 50 minutes*

INGREDIENTS

- **2 packages** (6 ounces each) wild rice, cooked according to package instructions
- ½ **teaspoon** salt
- 1 **teaspoon** black pepper
- ½ **teaspoon** paprika
- 1 **teaspoon** garlic powder
- 1 **tablespoon** butter
- 1 **teaspoon** canola oil
- **6 skinless**, boneless chicken breast halves
- **2 medium** shallots, minced
- **3 cups** sliced mushrooms
- 1 **tablespoon** cornstarch
- **3 tablespoons** water
- 1 **teaspoon** dried rosemary, crumbled
- 2½ **cups** low-sodium chicken stock (canned or homemade, see page 50)
- ⅔ **cup** dry sherry (see note)

1. PREHEAT the oven to 375°F.

2. COOK the wild rice according to the package directions. Spoon the rice into an ungreased 9 x 13-inch baking dish and set it aside.

3. SPRINKLE ¼ teaspoon of the salt, plus the pepper, paprika, and garlic powder on both sides of each chicken breast and set them aside.

4. HEAT the butter with the canola oil in a large, nonstick skillet over medium heat until the butter is melted. Add the chicken and cook it 4 minutes on each side. Place the chicken on top of the rice in the baking dish.

5. ADD the shallots and mushrooms to the same skillet and cook over medium heat, stirring frequently, for 5 minutes.

6. COMBINE the cornstarch and water in a small bowl. Add the cornstarch mixture to the skillet and stir until the sauce thickens slightly.

7. ADD the remaining ¼ teaspoon salt plus the flour and rosemary to the skillet, stirring to combine.

8. ADD the chicken stock and sherry to the skillet and cook for 3 minutes, stirring constantly, until the sauce is thickened and bubbly.

9. POUR the sauce over the chicken and rice in the baking dish. Cover the dish with foil and bake for 45 minutes. Serve immediately.

WHAT IS IT? WHERE DO I FIND IT?

DRY SHERRY Sherry is a wine that has been "fortified" with additional alcohol. Choose a high-quality brand of dry sherry from Spain at your local liquor shop. (Avoid using "cooking sherry"—it isn't very tasty.) Chefs like to keep sherry on hand because it adds great flavor to sauces and marinades.

penne with shrimp and feta

Pasta with a zesty Mediterranean flair

Serves: 4-6 ✳ *Prep time: 15-20 minutes* ✳ *Cooking time: 25*

INGREDIENTS

Vegetable oil cooking spray

- **4 tablespoons** olive oil
- **1 ½ pounds** flash-frozen, deveined shrimp, thawed (see page 159)
- **½ teaspoon** crushed red pepper flakes
- **1 ½ teaspoons** minced garlic
- **1 ¼ tablespoons** lime juice
- **¾ cup** white wine
- **4 cups** canned diced tomatoes, drained
- **1 teaspoon** dried dill or 2 tablespoons fresh dill, chopped
- **1 teaspoon** dried oregano
- salt and pepper, to taste
- **8 ounces** feta cheese, crumbled (see page 55)
- **1 pound** penne, cooked al dente and drained

1. **PREHEAT** the oven to 400°F. Coat a 13 x 9 x 2-inch baking pan with cooking spray.

2. **HEAT** 3 tablespoons of the olive oil in a large skillet over medium heat.

3. **ADD** the shrimp and red pepper flakes to the skillet and cook for 1 minute, stirring frequently. Use a slotted spoon to transfer the shrimp to the baking pan.

4. **HEAT** the remaining 1 tablespoon of olive oil in the same skillet over medium heat. Add the garlic and cook for 30 seconds. Add the lime juice, wine, tomatoes, dill, oregano, salt, and pepper; **SIMMER** for 8 to 10 minutes (a few pearl-sized bubbles will appear every minute). Remove the skillet from the heat.

5. **SPRINKLE** the feta cheese over the shrimp in the baking dish. Pour the tomato mixture over the feta-covered shrimp. Bake for 10 to 12 minutes. Remove the dish from the oven.

6. PLACE the penne in a large, warm serving bowl. Add the shrimp mixture to the bowl and toss until all the ingredients are blended. Serve immediately.

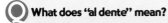

✳ **NOW WHAT?!** ✳

What does "al dente" mean?
This is an Italian phrase meaning "to the tooth" and refers to cooking pasta just until it resists slightly when bitten into.

6 Poultry

Chicken is a mainstay for dinner because it's fast, versatile, and easy to prepare. Why not add a little pizzazz to your meals with these easy gourmet chicken recipes? Choose from Pecan-Crusted Chicken (top), Chicken-Mushroom Quesadillas (middle), or Raspberry Chicken (bottom).

raspberry chicken

Boldly flavored, healthful, and pretty as a picture

Serves 6 ✳ *Prep time: 10 minutes* ✳ *Marinate: 2 hours or overnight* ✳
Cooking time: 35 minutes ✳

INGREDIENTS

Vegetable cooking oil spray

- **6** boneless, skinless chicken breast halves
- ½ **cup** seedless raspberry jam or fruit-only-style raspberry preserves
- ¼ **cup** orange juice
- ½ **cup** frozen pineapple juice concentrate, thawed
- ½ **cup** soy sauce
- **3 tablespoons** raspberry vinegar
- **2** large shallots, finely minced
- ½ **teaspoon** chili powder
- **1 teaspoon** garlic powder
- ½ **cup** fresh raspberries, mashed with fork

Garnish (optional):
- ½ **cup** fresh raspberries

1. **COAT** a large glass baking dish with vegetable oil cooking spray.

2. **PLACE** the chicken in the baking dish and set aside.

3. **COMBINE** all the remaining ingredients (except the garnish) in a medium-sized bowl.

4. **POUR** the marinade over the chicken and cover the baking dish tightly with foil.

5. **REFRIGERATE** the chicken for 2 hours, or overnight.

6. When you're ready to cook, **PREHEAT** the oven to 350°F.

7. **PLACE** the covered baking dish in the oven and bake for 30 minutes.

8. **REMOVE** the baking dish from the oven. Transfer the chicken to a warm serving platter. Pour some of the pan juices over the chicken. Serve the remaining juices in a small bowl if you wish.

9. **GARNISH** the platter with fresh raspberries and serve.

WHAT IS IT? WHERE DO I FIND IT?

RASPBERRY VINEGAR is voluptuous stuff—milder and fruitier than your usual vinegar, and slightly sweet. You'll find raspberry vinegar at most supermarkets or in gourmet shops. Unopened it will keep indefinitely; once opened, raspberry vinegar can be stored in a cool, dark place for up to six months.

What to serve with Raspberry Chicken? Try Sesame Asparagus (page 78) and Lemon-Dill Carrots (page 84).

chicken with honey mustard and basil

A sweet and savory marinade enhances the flavors of grilled chicken

Serves 6 ✳ *Prep time: 15 minutes* ✳ *Marinate: 20 minutes* ✳ *Cooking time: 8 minutes*

INGREDIENTS

- ⅔ **cup** dry white wine
- ¼ **cup** olive oil
- 3 **cloves** garlic, chopped
- 2½ **tablespoons** Dijon mustard
- 3 **tablespoons** soy sauce
- 3½ **tablespoons** honey
- ⅓ **cup** finely chopped fresh basil or 2 tablespoons dried
- 6 boneless, skinless chicken breast halves

1. COMBINE all the ingredients except the chicken in a large shallow dish and whisk until the marinade is thoroughly blended.

2. ADD the chicken breasts to the marinade, turning to coat them thoroughly.

3. MARINATE the chicken at room temperature for 20 minutes. (If you are not going to cook right away, you can marinate it in the refrigerator for up to 4 hours.)

4. Meanwhile, **PREPARE** a barbecue for medium-heat grilling, or preheat the oven broiler.

5. Remove the chicken breasts from the marinade and **TRANSFER** the marinade to a small saucepan. Place it over medium-high heat and bring the sauce to a **BOIL** (nickle-sized bubbles will form every few seconds). Boil for 1 minute; then reduce the heat and **SIMMER** the marinade (pearl-sized bubbles will form every few seconds) for 2 to 3 minutes, until it is reduced (cooked down) by half.

6. While the marinade is cooking, place the chicken on the grill or broiler pan. **GRILL** or broil the chicken about 4 minutes per side, or until it is cooked through (the juices will run clear when the chicken is pierced to the center of the thickest part with a fork or skewer).

7. PLACE the chicken on a warm serving platter and pour some of the marinade over it. Serve immediately.

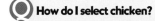

✹ **NOW WHAT?!** ✹

🔵 **How do I select chicken?**

Whether it's a whole bird or chicken parts you're buying, always check the "Sell by..." date to be sure the bird isn't past its prime. Choose meaty, full-breasted poultry. If there's skin, it should be intact, without bruises. Avoid poultry with an "off" odor or any package that is torn or leaking.

sesame chicken

Grill or bake it, either way it's a snap to prepare

Serves 4-6 ✳ *Prep time: 10 minutes* ✳ *Marinate: 4 hours* ✳ *Cooking time: 20 minutes on a grill; or 50 minutes in an oven*

INGREDIENTS

- ½ **cup** olive oil
- ⅔ **cup** dry sherry (see page 37)
- ½ **cup** soy sauce
- 6 **cloves** garlic, minced
- ¾ **teaspoon** ground ginger or 2 tablespoons grated fresh ginger
- 1 ½ **teaspoons** black pepper
- ⅔ **cup** chopped onions
- 1 **tablespoon** grated orange zest (see page 85)
- 4 **tablespoons** sesame seeds
- 2 **whole** chickens, quartered (You can purchase quartered chicken in packages at the supermarket.)

1. COMBINE all the ingredients except the chicken in a medium-sized bowl; stir the marinade well.

2. PLACE the chicken quarters in two large zip-top bags and divide the marinade evenly between them. Seal the bags and marinate chicken in the refrigerator for at least 4 hours (can be prepared one day in advance).

3. When you are ready to cook, **PREHEAT** the grill until the coals are very hot or preheat the oven to 450°F. Remove the chicken from bags, reserving the marinade in a medium-sized pan, and place the chicken on the grill or in a large roasting pan.

4. GRILL the chicken for 20 minutes, turning it and spooning a few tablespoons of the marinade over it every 4-5 minutes. (If you are using the oven, cook the chicken for 45-50 minutes, basting it every 8-10 minutes.)

5. Meanwhile, **PLACE** the pan of marinade over high heat and bring to a **BOIL** (nickle-sized bubbles will form). Boil for 1 minute; then reduce the heat to low, so that the marinade simmers for 3 minutes.

6. TEST the chicken to see if it's done by piercing the thigh deeply with a skewer or a sharp, narrow knife. If the juices running out of the puncture are clear (show no hint of pink), the chicken is done.

7. REMOVE the chicken quarters from the grill or the oven and place them on a heated plate. Pour the warm marinade over the chicken and serve. (This dish may also be served at room temperature or cooled in the refrigerator and served cold.)

✸ NOW WHAT? ✸

I've heard chicken harbors dangerous salmonella bacteria that can make people sick. How can I avoid that?
Wash thoroughly with soap and hot water anything—knives, hands, cutting board, countertop, sink—that comes into contact with raw chicken or its juices. Keep raw chicken refrigerated right up till you use it (preferably not more than one day, absolutely not more than two days). Never let it sit outside the refrigerator for more than half an hour before cooking. Cook chicken until no red or pink juices run out of the meat when the thickest part is pierced deeply with a fork or a skewer. If the juices are tinged with red or pink when tested or if the chicken is still slightly pink inside when it is cut at the table, return it to the grill or broiler to cook for a minute or two longer.

• • •

How do I baste?
Basting consists of pouring a flavorful liquid — usually a marinade or the liquid drippings in the bottom of the pan — over food while it is roasting (or broiling or grilling). To accomplish this all-important feat, use a spoon, a pastry or barbecue brush, or a bulb baster (a long tube with a bulb on top that sucks in liquid, which then can be squeezed out on the food). Basting moistens the food and adds flavor.

chicken-mushroom quesadillas

A great way to turn leftover chicken into a crowd-pleasing lunch

Serves 6-8 ✳ *Prep time: 20 minutes* ✳ *Cooking time: 20 minutes*

INGREDIENTS

- **3 tablespoons** butter
- **2 tablespoons** canola oil
- **4 cloves** garlic, minced
- **1 teaspoon** ground cumin
- **2 teaspoons** chili powder
- **1½ teaspoons** dried oregano
- **5 ounces** fresh shiitake mushrooms, stemmed and thinly sliced (about 1¼ cup)
- **5 ounces** button or white mushrooms, thinly sliced (about 1¼ cup)
- **2 cups** chopped cooked white-meat chicken
- **2½ tablespoons** lime juice
- **¾ cup** thinly sliced red onion
- **2 tablespoons** dried cilantro or ½ cup fresh cilantro
- **2¾ cups** shredded Monterey Jack cheese
- Salt and black pepper to taste
- Olive oil cooking spray
- **16** flour tortillas (5½ " round)

1. PLACE the butter and canola oil in a large skillet over medium-high heat. Swirl them together as the butter melts.

2. ADD the garlic, cumin, chili powder, and oregano; reduce the heat to low and cook for 1 minute, stirring constantly so that the food doesn't burn.

3. ADD the shiitake and button mushrooms; continue stirring and cooking until the mushrooms are tender, about 10 minutes.

4. REMOVE the skillet from the heat and mix in the chicken, lime juice, onion, and cilantro.

5. COOL the chicken mixture 10 to 15 minutes, then mix in the cheese, and salt and pepper to taste.

6. Meanwhile, **PREPARE** the barbecue grill (medium heat) or place a large, heavy skillet on the stove top on medium-high heat.

7. LIGHTLY SPRAY one side of 8 tortillas with olive oil cooking spray and place them, oiled side down, on a large baking sheet.

Serve these Chicken-Mushroom Quesadillas with salsa and you have a great lunch.

8. DIVIDE the chicken mixture evenly among the tortillas, spreading the mixture over them to within 1 inch of the edges.

9. TOP the chicken mixture with the remaining tortillas, pressing them down, and then spray them with oil.

10. Using a spatula, transfer the quesadillas to the hot grill and **GRILL** the quesadillas until lightly brown, about 3 minutes per side. If using the stove top, place the quesadillas in the skillet, one at a time, and cook them 2-3 minutes per side, until they are lightly browned; then transfer them to an oven-proof serving platter and keep them in a warm oven while cooking the remaining quesadillas.

11. COOL the quesadillas 30 seconds, then cut them into wedges with a pizza wheel or a sharp knife and serve immediately.

✳ **NOW WHAT?!** ✳

Q Can I buy chicken that's already cooked?

Yes. Look for packages of vacuum-packed pre-cooked chicken in the poultry section of your supermarket.

chicken parmesan

An Italian classic that warms the heart

Serves 4-6 ✳ *Prep time: 20 minutes* ✳ *Cooking time: 20 minutes*

INGREDIENTS

- **6** skinless, boneless chicken breast halves
- **⅔ cup** seasoned Italian bread crumbs
- **½ cup** grated Parmesan cheese
- **1 teaspoon** dried Italian seasonings
- **1 teaspoon** garlic powder
- **½ teaspoon** black pepper
- **¼ cup** all-purpose flour
- **3 large** egg whites
- **2 tablespoons** olive oil
- **3 cups** prepared tomato sauce
- **2 cups** shredded part-skim mozzarella cheese

1. POUND the chicken breasts (see opposite page).

2. COMBINE the next 6 ingredients in a shallow dish and stir the breadcrumb mixture well.

3. PLACE the egg whites in another shallow bowl and use a whisk or fork to beat them until they are slightly foamy.

4. DREDGE the chicken breasts, one at a time, in the breadcrumb mixture. Dip them in egg whites, and then again in the bread crumb mixture.

5. HEAT the oil in a large skillet over medium heat.

6. ADD the chicken breasts, a few at a time, arranging them in the skillet so that they do not touch. Cook the chicken for 5-6 minutes on each side, or until they are lightly browned.

7. SPOON enough tomato sauce into a large heat-proof ceramic baking dish to cover the bottom with a thin layer. Add the browned chicken breasts; spoon ½ cup tomato sauce over each breast and top it with ⅓ cup mozzarella cheese.

8. PREHEAT the broiler. Place the dish containing the chicken on a baking sheet.

9. BROIL the chicken 3 minutes, or until the cheese melts.

10. TRANSFER the chicken to a heated platter. Serve immediately.

✳ **NOW WHAT?!** ✳

How do I pound chicken?

Place the chicken breasts between sheets of wax paper or plastic wrap, and pound them with medium force, using the flat side of a meat mallet (sometimes called a meat tenderizer). If the utensil has two sides, use the flat part and not the spiky side, which might shred the chicken too much. If you do not have a meat mallet, the bottom of a skillet will do. Carefully wash any surface (including your hands) that touches the raw poultry, since it often carries dangerous salmonella bacteria.

• • •

How long will this dish keep?

You can prepare the whole thing ahead of time and simply freeze the finished, but uncooked, dish. When you are ready to cook, thaw and broil. Once cooked, it will keep in a sealed container in the refrigerator for up to 2 days.

• • •

I don't have any seasoned Italian bread crumbs. Will plain ones do?

In a pinch, yes, plain unflavored bread crumbs will do. You can compensate for their plainness by mixing in spices to season the bread crumbs. Try 1 teaspoon of dried oregano, 1 teaspoon of dried basil, and a dash of salt.

turkey meatloaf

It tastes like old-fashioned meatloaf, but it's much healthier, since it's lower in saturated fats

Serves 6-8 ✳ *Prep time: 15 minutes* ✳ *Cooking time: Approximately 1 hour and 10 minutes*

INGREDIENTS

2 ½ **pounds** ground turkey

1 **large** onion, chopped (about 1 ½ cups)

3 **cloves** garlic, minced

2 **extra-large** eggs, lightly beaten (or 3 egg whites)

2 **tablespoons** Worcestershire sauce

⅓ **cup** white wine

¼ **cup** plain bread crumbs or 1 slice of bread, torn into small pieces

1 ½ **teaspoons** salt

1 **teaspoon** black pepper

1 **teaspoon** dried thyme

⅔ **cup** ketchup

1. PREHEAT the oven to 375°F.

2. PLACE all the ingredients except the ketchup in a large bowl.

3. COMBINE the ingredients, using your hands to mix them thoroughly.

4. SHAPE the turkey mixture into a loaf and place it in a large baking dish. Spread the ketchup evenly over the top of the loaf.

5. BAKE the loaf for one hour and ten minutes; or until the meatloaf is cooked through (the juices show no hint of pink when the thickest part of the loaf is pierced deeply with a skewer or a small, sharp knife).

6. TRANSFER the loaf to a heated platter, cut it crosswise into slices, and serve. (The meatloaf also can be refrigerated and served cold in a sandwich.)

WHAT IS IT? WHERE DO I FIND IT?

GROUND TURKEY is now stocked in most supermarket poultry sections as a ground beef alternative. Handle it with the same care you would use for any poultry: carefully wash your hands, any surface, and any utensil that touches raw poultry, since the meat can contain salmonella bacteria. Buy the freshest package you can, and store it in the refrigerator, but never longer than two days. Don't worry too much, cooking thoroughly kills all the bacteria.

✹ NOW WHAT?! ✹

How do I prevent cracks in meatloaf?

Before baking the meatloaf, rub the top of it with cold water to smooth the surface and minimize cracking.

• • •

How do I get rid of grease in the meatloaf pan?

Use a bulb baster to remove grease from the pan as the meatloaf bakes. After it's cooked, pour any remaining grease in an empty can and throw away. Don't pour grease down the drain.

chicken with sun-dried tomatoes

A creamy classic that goes beautifully with pasta

Serves 4-6 ✳ *Prep time: 15 minutes* ✳ *Cooking time: 12 minutes*

INGREDIENTS

- **1 cup** yellow cornmeal
- **6** boneless, skinless chicken breast halves, cut into 1-inch strips
- **3 tablespoons** unsalted butter
- **2 tablespoons** olive oil
- **3 shallots,** minced
- **¾ cup** evaporated skim milk
- **⅔ cup** dry white wine
- **½ cup** chopped rehydrated sun-dried tomatoes (see page 17)
- salt and black pepper to taste
- **1-2 teaspoons** dried basil or 3 tablespoons chopped fresh basil

1. PLACE the cornmeal in medium-sized bowl; dredge (see page 137) the chicken with cornmeal until it's coated, shaking off the excess.

2. PLACE the butter and oil in a large heavy skillet over medium heat. Swirl the mixture until the butter melts.

3. ADD the chicken pieces to the skillet, a few at a time, and cook over medium heat, turning frequently, for 5 to 6 minutes, until the chicken is lightly browned on both sides. The chicken should be just cooked through (the strips will feel springy when pressed with your finger).

4. TRANSFER the chicken to a warm plate, using a slotted spoon.

5. ADD the shallots to the skillet and cook over low heat for 1 minute.

6. ADD the evaporated milk, white wine, sun-dried tomatoes, and salt and pepper. Bring the mixture to a **BOIL** (nickle-sized bubbles will form every few seconds).

7. REDUCE the heat to low and **SIMMER** (pearl-sized bubbles will form every few seconds), stirring frequently, for 4-5 minutes, or until the sauce thickens.

8. STIR in the basil.

9. RETURN the chicken to the skillet and cook for about 2 minutes, or until the chicken is just heated through. Adjust seasonings to taste, and transfer the chicken to a warm serving platter. Pour the sauce over it and serve immediately.

Beware of HiddenTreasures

It was my first time roasting a chicken. I got a nice 5-pound chicken, rinsed it, and patted it dry. Then I added some salt and pepper just like my sister had told me. I put it in a roasting pan and popped it in the oven. When it was done, it looked and smelled great. My girlfriend and I dug in. All was well until she noticed a piece of plastic. She pulled on it and out came a plastic bag of giblets. She said I was supposed to remove this before I cooked the chicken. Oh? Next time, I'll look inside and out.

Michael T., Bartlesville, Oklahoma

roast chicken

There's nothing tastier than a plump, perfectly roasted chicken with a light, citrusy gravy

Serves 4-6 ✳ *Prep time: 30 minutes* ✳ *Cooking time: 1 hour and 15 minutes*

INGREDIENTS

- 1 **5- to 6-pound** roasting chicken

  salt and black pepper
- 1 **tablespoon** dried thyme, or 4 sprigs fresh thyme
- 1 **tablespoon** dried rosemary, or 2 sprigs fresh rosemary
- 1 orange, quartered
- 1 lemon, quartered
- 4 **cloves** garlic, peeled
- 2 **tablespoons** softened butter

GRAVY

- ¾ **cup** low-sodium chicken broth
- 1 **tablespoon** cornstarch
- ¼ **cup** dry white wine
- ½ **cup** orange juice

for the chicken

1. PREHEAT the oven to 425°F. Get out a large roasting pan.

2. REMOVE the plastic bag of organs from the chicken's cavity and discard. Rinse the chicken (inside and out) under cold water and pat dry with paper towels.

3. SPRINKLE the cavity of the chicken with salt and pepper. Place the thyme, rosemary, orange, lemon, and garlic inside the cavity and rub them in. **TIE** the legs of the chicken together with kitchen twine to keep the cavity loosely closed.

4. RUB the outside of the chicken with butter and sprinkle the skin with salt and pepper.

5. PLACE the chicken in the roasting pan.

6. ROAST the chicken, basting every 10-15 minutes (see page 117), for 1 hour and 15 minutes, or until the juices run clear when you prick the inside thigh meat deeply with a small, sharp knife. Remove the chicken from the oven when no pink tinge can be detected in the juices. Untie the chicken legs; remove and discard the orange and lemon quarters.

7. TRANSFER the chicken to a warm platter and cover it with an aluminum foil tent to keep it warm while you prepare the gravy.

for the gravy

1. ADD the chicken broth to the roasting pan; place it over medium-high heat. Stir for 3-4 minutes, deglazing the bottom of the pan (see note at right).

2. In a small bowl, **MIX** the cornstarch with 2 tablespoons of warm broth from the pan. Use a whisk to combine the mixture well, and then add it to the pan, blending constantly with the whisk until it is smooth.

3. BRING the mixture to a **BOIL** (nickle-sized bubbles will form every few seconds), and then reduce heat so that it **SIMMERS** (pearl-sized bubbles will form every few seconds). Stir in the white wine and orange juice.

4. POUR the gravy through a strainer into a gravy bowl. (The strainer will catch any lumps or bits of chicken.) Season it to taste with salt and pepper. Serve with the chicken.

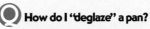

✳ **NOW WHAT?!** ✳

🔘 **How do I "deglaze" a pan?**

Deglazing means adding a little liquid to a pan in which meat or poultry has been cooked, heating it to a boil, and stirring to loosen the browned bits of food still clinging to the pan. The resulting meaty liquid can be used as a sauce or as a basis for gravy. Before deglazing, pour most of the grease left from cooking into an empty coffee can and discard it. Too much grease will make your gravy or sauce too oily.

pecan-crusted chicken

Moist on the inside, crisp on the outside

Serves 6 ✳ *Prep time: 20 minutes* ✳ *Marinate: 30 minutes* ✳
Cooking time: 30 minutes

INGREDIENTS

MARINADE

3 tablespoons sesame oil

2 tablespoons canola or vegetable oil

2 teaspoons dry sherry

2 tablespoons minced shallots

½ teaspoon grated lemon zest (see page 85)

½ teaspoon grated lime zest (see page 85)

I tablespoon lemon juice

I tablespoon lime juice

I teaspoon black pepper

Vegetable oil cooking spray

for the marinade

I. WHISK together all the ingredients in a small bowl. Set aside.

for the chicken

I. PREHEAT the oven to 450°F.

2. PLACE the chicken breasts in a shallow glass dish. Pour the marinade over the breasts and turn each one to coat it thoroughly. Cover the dish with plastic wrap and refrigerate it for 20 to 30 minutes.

3. COMBINE all the remaining ingredients, except the butter, in the bowl of a food processor or a blender. Process the mixture in short bursts until the crackers have turned to crumbs and the pecans are broken into tiny pieces. Pour the crumb mixture into a shallow bowl.

4. SPRAY a shallow roasting pan with vegetable oil cooking spray.

5. **REMOVE** the chicken from the marinade and discard marinade.

6. **COAT** both sides of the chicken breasts with the crumb mixture and place them in the roasting pan.

7. **DRIZZLE** the chicken with the melted butter and place it in the oven. Roast for 30 minutes, until the chicken is crisp and browned.

8. **REMOVE** the chicken from the oven. Transfer it to a warm platter and serve. (The chicken can be refrigerated and served cold.)

CHICKEN	
6	skinless, boneless chicken breast halves, washed and patted dry
1	**cup** crushed wheat crackers, such as wheat thins or stoned wheat thins
⅔	**cup** grated Parmesan cheese
2	**teaspoons** dried basil, or ¼ **cup** chopped fresh basil
1	**teaspoon** dried parsley
1	**teaspoon** garlic powder
1	**teaspoon** black pepper
⅔	**cup** pecans
¼	**cup** melted butter

Crunchy and bursting with flavor, Pecan-Crusted Chicken makes a lovely dinner. Serve with Wild Rice Salad, see page 60.

7 Meats

Try these hearty favorites for your next main course. From top to bottom: Mom's Meatloaf, Lamb Chops with Pesto, and Veal Paprika.

caribbean pork tenderloins

The pan drippings provide a nice base for a quick sauce

Serves 6-8 ✳ *Prep time: 15 minutes* ✳ *Marinate: overnight*
✳ *Cooking time: 30 minutes*

INGREDIENTS

½ **cup** orange juice
½ **cup** lime juice
½ **cup** dark rum
¼ **cup** pineapple juice
6 **cloves** garlic, minced
1 **large** onion, chopped
2 **teaspoons** ground ginger
2 **teaspoons** dried oregano
1 **teaspoon** dried basil
2 **teaspoons** dried cumin
2 bay leaves, crumbled
1 **teaspoon** salt
1 **teaspoon** black pepper
4 pork tenderloins, 12 ounces each, rinsed and patted dry
½ **cup** chicken broth
1 **tablespoon** flour

1. **MIX** the orange juice, ¼ cup of the lime juice, ¼ cup of the dark rum, and the next 10 ingredients in a large bowl to make a marinade. Divide it among four large zip-top plastic bags.

2. **ADD** a pork tenderloin to each bag and close it securely. Turn the bags so that the pork is coated with the marinade.

3. **REFRIGERATE** the bagged pork loins overnight.

4. When ready to cook, **PREHEAT** the oven to 400°F.

5. **PLACE** the tenderloins in a roasting pan large enough so the pork loins can fit without touching each other. Discard the marinade.

6. **ROAST** the pork for 25-30 minutes, or until a thermometer inserted into the center registers 150°F. Remove the pork from the pan and place it on a serving platter. Make a tent with aluminum foil and place it over the pork to keep it warm while it "rests" for a few minutes.

7. While the meat is resting, **PLACE** the roasting pan on top of stove and turn the heat to medium.

8. **ADD** the remaining lime juice and rum to the pan. Stir the mixture as it begins to bubble, scraping up the pan drippings from the bottom of the pan.

9. **ADD** the chicken broth and flour to the pan. Use a whisk to combine the flour mixture thoroughly with the pan drippings mixture. Continue whisking vigorously as the mixture boils (nickle-sized bubbles will form every few seconds).

10. **COOK** 2 minutes at a boil, or until the sauce is slightly thickened, whisking to keep it smooth. Remove the sauce from the heat.

11. **SLICE** the pork crosswise into ½-inch-thick slices and serve with some of the sauce drizzled over it. The remainder can be served alongside the meat in a gravy dish.

✳ **NOW WHAT?!** ✳

🔘 **What does it mean to allow meat to "rest"?**

That's when you delay cutting meat for a few minutes after taking it from the oven. During this time the juices settle into the meat fiber. Without this resting period, the juices run out too freely when the meat is cut, and some of the flavor leaches away.

• • •

🔘 **I don't have any aluminum foil. Can I let the roast rest uncovered?**

A tinfoil tent keeps the roast from cooling too much while it rests. In a pinch, make a tent from a torn-open paper bag or several layers of newspaper.

beef tenderloin

Simply roast and serve hot, cold, or at room temperature. Do not overcook—it's best when pink

Serves 8 ✳ *Prep time: 15 minutes* ✳ *Cooking time: 40 minutes*

INGREDIENTS

- 1 **3-pound** beef tenderloin, trimmed and tied, at room temperature
- 2 **tablespoons** butter, softened
- 1 **tablespoon** black pepper
- 1 **teaspoon** salt

SAUCE

- 1 **tablespoon** olive oil
- 1 **tablespoon** butter
- ¼ **cup** chopped onions or scallions
- 2 **tablespoons** minced shallots
- 1½ **teaspoons** Dijon mustard
- 1 **teaspoon** dried parsley or 1 tablespoon minced fresh parsley
- ¾ **cup** dry sherry (see page 37)

1. **PREHEAT** the oven to 450°F.

2. **RUB** the butter over the tenderloin, then rub in the pepper and salt. Place it in a shallow roasting pan.

3. **ROAST** the tenderloin for 35 minutes. Remove from oven and cover the meat with a tinfoil tent. Let the roast stand, or rest, for 10 to 15 minutes before carving.

4. While the tenderloin is resting, **HEAT** the olive oil and butter in a small skillet until the butter has melted. **ADD** the onions and shallots to the skillet and cook over medium-high heat, stirring frequently so the mixture won't burn, about 3 to 4 minutes.

5. **ADD** the mustard, parsley, and sherry and bring the mixture to a boil (nickle-sized bubbles will form every few seconds). Remove the pan from heat.

6. **CARVE** the beef into 1-inch-thick slices and dribble some of the sauce over it.

WHAT IS IT? WHERE DO I FIND IT?

BEEF TENDERLOIN is a choice, boneless cut taken from along the backbone of the cow. Buy it from a reputable butcher to get the best quality. You might want to purchase a whole tenderloin (6 to 8 pounds prior to trimming), and have the butcher cut half of it off to roast and then slice the rest into 1-inch-thick slabs for steaks (called filet mignon). Wrap the steaks individually in plastic wrap, then aluminum foil. Label them with the date and place them in the freezer.

☀ NOW WHAT?! ☀

Q Is trimmed tenderloin better?

You can buy tenderloin untrimmed, with the fat on, or trimmed, with the fat removed by a butcher. The price per pound is higher for trimmed, but it's worth it. Before roasting, use kitchen twine or string to tie the meat at intervals of 2 to 3 inches, so that the tenderloin will hold together while roasting and will cook evenly.

FIRST PERSON DISASTER

All tied up

Time is money and I try to conserve both. I have a lot of things on my plate and have to plan everything down to the minute. When I planned a dinner party, my first in a long time, I bought an expensive beef tenderloin and asked the butcher to trim and tie it up for me to save time. I prepared it according to the recipe and put it into the oven and had a drink with my guests. We were ready for dinner just as the oven bell chimed. I pulled the beef out and put it on the platter for a few moments to rest while I brought out the already prepared side dishes. I carried in the tenderloin and my husband cut it into slices and served everyone. We all dug in...that's when I saw the first of my guests gently tugging the twine off her meat. In my haste I'd forgotten to take off the twine! Well, it had turned brown in the cooking and practically blended right into the meat. Clearly, time well spent is more important than being on time.

Pat V., Saratoga, New York

veal paprika

A creamy, soothing, flavorful dish

Serves 6 ✳ *Prep time: 15 minutes* ✳ *Cooking time: 30 minutes*

INGREDIENTS

6 tablespoons canola or vegetable oil

1 ½ pounds veal scallops (¼-inch thick)

1 cup flour seasoned with salt and pepper for dredging (see next page)

2 medium onions, thinly sliced

3 cloves garlic, finely minced

2 tablespoons plus 1 teaspoon sweet paprika

1 ½ cups light sour cream

1 ½ cups chicken broth

¾ cup dry sherry (see page 37) or dry white wine

1 tablespoon lemon juice

Garnish (optional): minced fresh parsley

1. **HEAT** 4 tablespoons of the oil in a large skillet over medium heat.

2. **DREDGE** the veal in seasoned flour and cook, in batches, in the skillet until the meat is lightly browned, 2 to 3 minutes on each side. Place the meat on a serving platter as each batch is browned. Add more oil to the skillet if it seems dry.

3. In same skillet, **SAUTÉ** the onions (cook over medium-high heat, turning them frequently so they won't burn) until golden, about 3 to 4 minutes.

4. **ADD** the garlic, paprika, 1 cup of the sour cream, the chicken broth, and the sherry to the skillet. Bring the mixture to a **BOIL** (nickle-sized bubbles will form every few seconds), stirring constantly with a whisk. Add the veal to the skillet and **SIMMER** (pearl-sized bubbles form) for about 5 minutes, or until the meat is tender.

5. **STIR** in the remaining sour cream, and the lemon juice. Add salt and pepper to taste. Place the veal on a serving plate and pour the sauce over it. Garnish with parsley, if desired, and serve.

Serve Veal Paprika and its savory sauce with Sweet Potato Gratin (see page 88).

WHAT IS IT? WHERE DO I FIND IT?

SWEET PAPRIKA is a bright-orange spice made from finely ground red peppers. It can be found in the spice aisle of any supermarket. The most flavorful type comes from Hungary, where foods flavored with paprika are a way of life. To retain the delicate flavor of paprika, keep it in the refrigerator after opening.

✳ NOW WHAT?! ✳

What is "dredging?"

It's coating a food lightly, usually with flour or cornmeal. Either place the coating mixture on a plate and dip the meat in it, or put it in a large plastic zip-top bag, add the meat in batches, then close and shake the bag.

veal scallops with mushrooms

A dinner party favorite—serve with pasta or rice

Serves 4-6 ✳ *Prep time: 20 minutes* ✳ *Cooking time: 20 minutes*

INGREDIENTS

- 1 ½ **pounds** veal scallops
- 1 **teaspoon** salt
- 1 **teaspoon** pepper
- ¼ **teaspoon** cayenne
- 4 **tablespoons** olive oil
- 4 **tablespoons** minced shallots
- 1 **cup** chicken broth
- ⅓ **cup** dry vermouth
- 1 ¼ **cup** sliced fresh mushrooms
- 2 **teaspoons** dried chives
- 1 **tablespoon** dried tarragon
- 1 **tablespoon** dried parsley
- 3 **tablespoons** lemon juice
- 2 **tablespoons** butter

1. Place the veal scallops between two sheets of plastic wrap and **POUND** them, using the flat side of a meat mallet or the back of a heavy skillet, until they are about ⅛-inch thick. Remove the plastic wrap and discard it.

2. **SEASON** the veal with the salt, pepper, and cayenne.

3. **HEAT** the oil in a large skillet over medium-high heat. Add the veal to the skillet in batches, **SAUTÉ** each piece over medium-high heat, for 30 seconds on each side. Transfer the veal to a warm plate as soon as it turns slightly brown.

4. **ADD** the shallots to the remaining oil and juices in the skillet. Sauté for about 2 minutes over medium-high heat, stirring frequently to prevent them from scorching.

5. **ADD** the chicken broth to the skillet and scrape up any brown bits with a spatula or wooden spoon, mixing them into the broth. Add all the remaining ingredients except the butter, and **SIMMER** (pearl-sized bubbles will form every few seconds) until the mixture is reduced by half.

6. **ADD** the butter to the skillet, swirling it around until it has melted.

7. RETURN the veal with its juices to the skillet. Turn the veal to coat it with the sauce. Place the veal on a serving platter and drizzle the sauce over it and serve.

lamb chops with pesto

Equally delicious with homemade or prepared pesto

Serves 6 ✳ *Prep time: 10 minutes* ✳ *Cooking time: 10 minutes*

INGREDIENTS

- **1 cup** prepared or homemade pesto (see below)
- **8 tablespoons** plain, fat-free yogurt

Salt and pepper to taste

- **12** lean lamb loin chops on the bone (3 ounces each)

HOMEMADE PESTO

- **2 cups** fresh basil leaves, rinsed and thoroughly dried
- **3 cloves** garlic
- **2½ tablespoons** pine nuts
- **½ cup** grated Parmesan cheese
- **2 tablespoons** olive oil

1. STIR the yogurt into the pesto. Add salt and pepper.

2. PREHEAT the broiler or grill. Place the chops on the grill rack or broiler pan and broil them 4 minutes. Turn the chops over.

3. SPREAD the pesto mixture over the chops and broil 3 more minutes. (The chops will be medium rare.) Transfer the chops to a heated platter and serve.

for the homemade pesto

1. PLACE basil, garlic, pine nuts, and Parmesan cheese in the bowl of a food processor or blender; blend the ingredients till smooth.

2. ADD the olive oil, 2 teaspoons at a time, and continue blending until all the oil is incorporated.

WHAT IS IT? WHERE DO I FIND IT?

PESTO is a sauce served over pasta or meat, or added to thicken soups. It's made from basil, garlic, and Parmesan or Romano cheese in olive oil, and augmented with pine nuts or walnuts. Traditionally the ingredients are ground together using a mortar and pestle until they form a bright green paste, and then olive oil is slowly added into the mixture. Modern food processors make quick work of this chore. Prepared pesto is often found in refrigerator cases in supermarkets and specialty food stores.

Dress up your lamb chops with delicious pesto sauce. Serve the lamb on the bone or sliced (both ways are shown here).

flank steak

The meat has to marinate overnight, so plan ahead

Serves 6 ✳ *Prep time: 10 minutes* ✳ *Marinate: 12 hours*
✳ *Cooking time: 12 minutes*

INGREDIENTS

- ¾ **cup** soy sauce
- ½ **cup** olive oil
- 4 scallions, minced
- 6 **cloves** garlic, minced
- 2 **teaspoons** ground ginger or 2 tablespoons grated fresh ginger (see page 39)
- 5 **tablespoons** honey
- 1 **tablespoon** dried rosemary
- 2 **tablespoons** black pepper
- 1 **teaspoon** salt
- 1 **2-pound** flank steak

1. COMBINE all the ingredients except the steak in a large, flat, glass or ceramic baking dish.

2. ADD the steak to the marinade mixture and turn it until it is thoroughly coated.

3. COVER the dish tightly with plastic wrap and refrigerate overnight, turning the steak once or twice.

4. When ready to cook, **PREHEAT** a grill or broiler. Remove the steak from the marinade and discard the marinade.

5. GRILL (or broil) the steak to the desired degree of doneness, about 5 minutes per side for medium-rare.

6. TRANSFER the steak to a cutting surface, cover it with a aluminum foil tent, and let it rest for five minutes.

7. SLICE the steak across the grain into thin strips. Serve immediately or keep warm in an oven at 200° F.

WHAT IS IT? WHERE DO I FIND IT?

FLANK STEAK is a boneless cut of beef that's frequently marinated because it is not naturally very tender, although it is quite flavorful (some people consider it the most flavorful cut of beef). An oil-and-vinegar or an oil-and-soy-sauce marinade tenderizes the meat by dissolving some of the connective tissue in the fiber of the meat.

* NOW WHAT?! *

How do I cut flank steak?

Cut it across the grain at a 45-degree angle. If you cut it with the grain, it will be too chewy.

mom's meatloaf

A true blue plate special that is sure to please— the leftovers are great for sandwiches

Serves 6-8 ✹ *Prep time: 20 minutes* ✹ *Cooking time: 1 hour and 15 minutes*

INGREDIENTS

- **2 pounds** lean ground beef
- **½ pound** ground pork or veal
- **1 cup** chopped onion
- **2 teaspoons** minced garlic
- **2 eggs**, lightly beaten
- **¼ cup** ketchup or chili sauce
- **¼ cup** bread crumbs or 1 slice of bread torn into shreds
- **¼ cup** plain, nonfat yogurt or skim milk
- **2 tablespoons** Worcestershire sauce
- **2 teaspoons** dried thyme
- **1 teaspoon** dried basil
- **1 teaspoon** dried oregano
- **1 teaspoon** salt
- **1 teaspoon** black pepper

1. PREHEAT the oven to 350°F.

2. COMBINE all the ingredients in a large bowl, using your hands to mix everything together thoroughly.

3. PACK the mixture into a 9 x 5 x 3-inch loaf pan, or shape the mixture into a loaf and place it in a larger baking dish. Pour additional ketchup or chili sauce over the top of the loaf if you wish.

4. BAKE the meatloaf until it is firm to the touch in the center, about 1 hour and 15 minutes.

5. TRANSFER the loaf to a platter. Cut it crosswise into slices and serve.

WHAT IS IT? WHERE DO I FIND IT?

BREAD CRUMBS are ground dried bread. You can make your own by toasting stale bread and then grinding it in a blender or food processor. The easier solution is to buy them already prepared. They are sold in canisters; look for them in the condiment or bread section of your supermarket. You can use either plain or seasoned bread crumbs.

For serious comfort food try a slice of Mom's Meatloaf with Garlic Mashed Potatoes (see page 87).

(see page 87)

☀ **NOW WHAT?!** ☀

How do I prevent the top of my meatloaf from cracking?

You can rub water over the top of the loaf before baking.

• • •

Can I use other ground meats besides hamburger?

Meatloaf is any ground meat that has been bound together with eggs, yogurt, or milk. Any ground meat will do. Try creating combinations with ground beef, veal, pork, and turkey.

meat spaghetti sauce

A homemade hearty tomato sauce to serve over pasta

Serves 8 ✳ *Prep time: 30 minutes* ✳ *Cooking time: 1 hour*

INGREDIENTS

- **2 tablespoons** olive oil
- **3** 4-inch-long sweet Italian sausages (see variations at end of recipe)
- **3** 4-inch-long hot Italian sausages
- **2 pounds** lean ground beef
- **1 ½ cups** diced onions
- **6 cloves** garlic, minced
- **2 cans** (35 ounces each) Italian plum tomatoes, with juice
- **1 can** (28 ounces) crushed tomatoes, with juice
- **¾ cup** tomato paste
- **¾ cup** dry red wine
- **1 cup** canned tomato sauce
- **3 tablespoons** dried parsley
- **1 tablespoon** dried thyme
- **1 tablespoon** dried oregano
- **2 teaspoons** dried basil
- **1 teaspoon** black pepper
- **1 teaspoon** salt
- **1 pound (16 ounces)** pasta

1. HEAT the olive oil in a large skillet over medium heat.

2. REMOVE the sausages from their casings and break them into small pieces. Add the sausage meat to the pan and cook over medium-high heat, stirring frequently, until browned, about 10 minutes. Transfer the sausage to a colander and drain it. Put meat into a large, heavy pot and set aside.

3. ADD the ground beef to the skillet and **COOK** over medium-high heat, breaking the meat into small pieces and stirring it until lightly browned. Using a slotted spoon, transfer the ground beef to the pot with the sausage.

4. ADD the onions and garlic to the skillet and cook over medium heat for 2 to 3 minutes, stirring occasionally. Add them to the pot with the meat.

5. ADD the remaining ingredients, except the pasta, to the pot and bring the mixture to a **BOIL** on medium-high heat (nickle-sized bubbles will form every few seconds). Reduce the heat to low, and **SIMMER** for 45 minutes to 1 hour (pearl-sized bubbles will form every few seconds). Stir the mixture occasionally to prevent the sauce from sticking to the bottom of the pot.

6. COOK the pasta according to the directions on the package while the sauce is simmering. Drain the pasta thoroughly. Transfer it to a large heated bowl or platter and drizzle a little more olive oil over it.

7. ADJUST sauce seasonings to taste and pour over the pasta.

Variations If you don't have sausages handy or don't like them, substitute an additional pound of ground meat.

Add mushrooms, sweet bell peppers, or summer squash to vary the flavor and texture of the sauce.

Pasta with meat sauce is traditionally garnished with freshly grated Parmesan cheese.

Storage tip: Sauce will keep in the freezer for up to 6 months.

WHAT IS IT? WHERE DO I FIND IT?

ITALIAN SAUSAGES Sweet Italian sausage is traditionally made from highly seasoned ground pork flavored with garlic and sometimes fennel. Hot Italian sausage is similar, except it also has flakes of hot pepper in the mix. Find both at specialty butcher shops, supermarket meat cases, or Italian grocers. Both types are sold raw, and must be cooked thoroughly before eating.

Seafood

So flavorful and so good for you. Try these seafood delights—Shrimp and Leek Stir-Fry (top); and Crab Cakes (bottom).

crab cakes

A healthful version of an all-time favorite

Serves 4-6 ✳ *Prep time: 30 minutes* ✳ *Cooking time: 10 minutes*

INGREDIENTS

- **1 pound** crabmeat, pulled into shreds, or 16 ounces canned crabmeat (remove any bits of shell, see page 151)
- **3 tablespoons** nonfat plain yogurt
- **1½ tablespoons** Dijon mustard
- **2 tablespoons** scallions, minced (both white and green parts)
- **1 teaspoon** dried parsley
- **1** large egg, lightly beaten
- **1 teaspoon** salt
- **1 teaspoon** black pepper
- **1-2 dashes** Tabasco sauce
- **6 tablespoons plain** bread crumbs (see page 144)
- **½ -¾ cup** corn flakes, crushed
- **2 tablespoons** olive oil

1. PLACE all the ingredients except the corn flakes and olive oil in a large bowl and mix them together. Place the cornflakes on a piece of wax paper and crush with a rolling pin. Set aside.

2. FORM the crab mixture into 6 large cakes or 12 small flat cakes.

3. PRESS each side of the cakes into the cornflakes so that they are well coated; as you finish coating them, place each cake on a cutting board or a sheet of waxed paper. (The cakes can be prepared up to this point and kept in the refrigerator for up to 3 hours before cooking. Or they can be wrapped tightly in plastic wrap, placed in a sealed container, and kept in the freezer for up to 3 weeks.)

4. When ready to cook the crab cakes, **HEAT** the olive oil in a large skillet over medium-high heat.

5. SAUTÉ the cakes (cook over medium-high heat, checking frequently so the cakes won't burn) for about 5 minutes on each side, pressing down lightly with a spatula. Serve immediately.

☀ **NOW WHAT?!** ☀

🔵 **I don't have corn flakes on hand. Can I use another cereal?**
Yes. Any crisp, flaky cereal that is not sweetened will do as well.

• • •

🔵 **I don't want to serve the traditional tartar sauce with these cakes. What else would be good with them?**
A little salsa or tomato relish makes a nice garnish for crab cakes.

Crab Cakes are easier to make than most people think. Best of all, you can freeze them before cooking; just thaw and cook for a quick gourmet dinner.

WHAT IS IT? WHERE DO I FIND IT?

FRESH CRABMEAT You can find fresh crabmeat in the seafood section of most supermarkets or your local fish market. It's usually sold by the pound and is ready to use.

• • •

PREPARED CRABMEAT is also sold in cans like tuna fish. You should pick through the meat before using it and take out any stray bits of shell that may have been included during the processing of the crabmeat.

orange-pecan sea bass

Crunchy and citrusy—this woos many who shy away from seafood

Serves 4-6 ✳ *Prep time: 10 minutes* ✳ *Cooking time: 8-10 minutes*

INGREDIENTS

- **3 tablespoons** Dijon mustard
- **⅔ cup** orange juice
- **1 teaspoon** dried basil
- **1½ pounds** sea bass fillets
- salt and black pepper to taste
- flour for coating fillets
- **2 tablespoons** butter
- **1 tablespoon** canola oil
- **2 tablespoons** orange zest (see note)
- **⅔ cup** chopped pecans, toasted (see note)

1. **COMBINE** mustard, orange juice, and basil in a small bowl. Set aside.

2. **SEASON** fish fillets with salt and pepper.

3. **DREDGE** fillets in flour and shake off any excess.

4. **MELT** butter with oil in a large skillet over medium-high heat.

5. **ADD** fillets and cook until lightly browned, about 3 to 4 minutes per side.

6. **POUR** reserved orange juice mixture over fish and stir around fillets, scraping up any browned bits.

7. **COVER** pan and cook for 5 minutes.

8. **TRANSFER** to individual plates and sprinkle with orange zest and toasted pecans.

WHAT IS IT? WHERE DO I FIND IT?

ORANGE ZEST is a colorful and flavorful addition to a dish. You can't buy zest, you must make it by grating the skin of an orange. Use the back of a cheese grater and a freshly washed orange. Grate over a plate. The tiny particles are called zest. Avoid scraping into the pith, the white part of the peel; it adds a bitter taste.

❋ NOW WHAT?! ❋

What other fish might be substituted for sea bass?

Snapper or grouper will work in this recipe.

• • •

How do I toast chopped pecans?

First, chop the pecans. (You don't want to chop them after they are cooked as they will be too hot to handle.) Preheat the oven or toaster oven to 350°F. Place the nuts on a baking pan and toast for 12 minutes, stirring with a wooden spoon every few minutes so they cook evenly. Keep an eye on them so they don't burn.

d swordfish

...ine marinade complements the richness of the fish

Serves 6 ✳ *Prep time: 10 minutes* ✳ *Marinate: 2 to 4 hours* ✳ *Cooking time: 10 minutes*

INGREDIENTS

- ½ **cup** lime juice
- ¾ **cup** dry white wine
- 3 **cloves** garlic, minced
- 2 **tablespoons** Dijon mustard
- 3 **tablespoons** dried cilantro or parsley or ½ cup chopped fresh cilantro
- 2 **tablespoons** olive oil
- 1 **teaspoon** black pepper
- 6 swordfish steaks (about ⅓ to ½ pound each) 1-inch thick

1. PLACE all the ingredients except for the swordfish in a medium-sized bowl. Use a whisk to thoroughly blend the marinade.

2. ARRANGE the swordfish steaks in a large shallow glass dish and pour the marinade over them. Cover the dish with plastic wrap and refrigerate for 2 to 4 hours.

3. PREPARE a grill or preheat the broiler. Remove the fish from the marinade, reserving the liquid. Grill or broil the steaks for about 4 minutes on each side, or until the center is just opaque when you insert a small, sharp knife. Transfer the fish to a warm serving platter.

4. PLACE the remaining marinade in a small saucepan over medium heat and **BOIL** (pearl-sized bubbles will appear every few seconds) for a full minute.

5. POUR some of the cooked marinade over the fish and serve immediately.

Q Can I cook with left-over wine?

Yes, if it is a dry, white wine—which is best with fish—and if it is a good wine. But taste it first to see if it is still palatable. Never cook with any wine or spirit you wouldn't want to drink. Cooking intensifies the taste of wine, so use a good one.

• • •

Q Is it true you should never serve the marinade as a sauce?

You should never serve any uncooked marinade as a sauce because it is full of bacteria from the raw food that has been soaking in it. Cooked marinade is another story. To kill any latent bacteria, bring the marinade to a boil and keep it boiling for a full minute before serving.

WHAT IS IT? WHERE DO I FIND IT?

CILANTRO Also called fresh coriander, this tangy green herb looks a bit like Italian parsley, but its taste is much more pungent. You can find it in the produce sections of most supermarkets. Look for the freshest bunch because it does not keep for long.

baked tuna with sautéed vegetables

An updated version of the traditional "parchment" method of cooking, using aluminum foil instead

Serves 6 ✳ *Prep time: 15 minutes* ✳ *Cooking time: 6 to 8 minutes*

INGREDIENTS

- **3 tablespoons** olive oil
- **3** red bell peppers, seeded and thinly sliced
- **6** cloves garlic, minced
- **2 cups** snow peas, thinly sliced lengthwise, or green beans cut into 1-inch pieces, or 2 cups green peas
- **6** scallions, white and green parts, thinly sliced, or 1 small onion, diced
- **1 teaspoon** dried oregano
- **½ teaspoon** dried thyme
- **6** tuna steaks, 8 ounces each, about 1 inch thick
- **6 sheets** aluminum foil, each measuring 12 x 18 inches
- **3 tablespoons** butter

Salt and black pepper to taste

1. PREHEAT the oven to 425°F.

2. HEAT the oil in a large skillet over medium heat. Add the red pepper and **SAUTÉ** (cook over medium-high heat, checking frequently so the peppers won't burn) for 2 minutes.

3. ADD the garlic, snow peas, scallions, oregano, and thyme and sauté for 1 minute more. Remove pan from heat.

4. PLACE each of the tuna steaks in the center of a foil sheet. Top the steaks with equal amounts of the cooked vegetables. Place ½ tablespoon butter on top of the vegetables, then a sprinkle of salt and pepper.

5. FOLD the foil over each fish steak, bringing two opposite edges together to make a ridge across the top of the steak. Fold over the ridge twice so that it seals the foil packet. Place the packets on a baking sheet.

6. BAKE the fish packets 6 to 8 minutes for medium-rare tuna. Place the packets on a serving dish or on individual dinner plates. Open the packets slightly to let some of the steam escape. Serve immediately.

Why should tuna be cooked medium-rare?

Although tuna is tender and firm in texture and rich in flavor, it can become gray, chewy, and rather tasteless if it is cooked too long. It profits from a marinade, even if it is just a squeeze of lemon juice and fresh herbs.

• • •

I haven't heard of the traditional "parchment" method of cooking. What is it?

Parchment—a paper specially treated for cooking—was once commonly used to make packets in which fish or chicken was steamed along with aromatic herbs and vegetables. The process is often referred to on menus or in cookbooks by the French phrase "en papillote." Parchment is usually available in cookware specialty shops and some supermarkets.

FIRST PERSON DISASTER

It's all in the packaging

No sooner had I finished putting the vegetables on top of the fish, when the phone rang. It was the car mechanic. It's a cordless phone, so I could talk while I worked. The repair on my car turned out to be twice as much as the estimate! I was fuming. I quickly folded up the packets and put them in the oven. Then I called my husband with the bad news. When the oven buzzer beeped, I took the packets out and noticed some burnt liquid on the baking sheet. A peek inside told me the worst— the vegetables looked totally dried-up and the tuna was ashen. Apparently, three of the packets had not been sealed tightly enough, so the fish and vegetables were baked instead of steamed. I had to laugh—talk about letting off steam! My mom once told me "Never cook when you're mad." Now I understand why.

Mary Beth M., St. Augustine, Florida

shrimp and leek stir-fry

Sweet and spicy, it's best when made at the last minute

Serves 4-6 ✳ *Prep time: 20 minutes* ✳ *Cooking time: About 12 minutes*

INGREDIENTS

- **4 tablespoons** pine nuts
- **4 tablespoons** canola oil
- **5 leeks**, white and pale-green parts only, washed well and sliced into thin rounds
- **4 cloves** garlic, minced
- **1 teaspoon** ground ginger, or **1 tablespoon** minced fresh ginger (see page 39)
- **3 pounds** large frozen deveined shrimp, thawed (see note)
- **⅓ cup** dry sherry
- **⅓ cup** soy sauce
- **⅓ cup** orange juice
- **1 tablespoon** sesame oil
- **1 teaspoon** dried red pepper flakes (omit if you don't like spicy food)
- **3 cups** cooked white or brown rice

1. PREHEAT the oven to 350°F. Place the pine nuts in a shallow pan and put it into the oven for about 5 minutes, or until the nuts are lightly toasted. Be sure to watch them carefully or they will burn. Remove from oven and set aside.

2. HEAT the canola oil in a skillet over high heat.

3. ADD the leeks and **STIR-FRY** (cook over high heat, stirring constantly so the leeks won't burn) for about 3 minutes, or until they are just tender.

4. ADD the garlic and ginger and continue stir-frying for about half a minute. Add the shrimp and stir-fry until they turn pink and are heated through, about 1 minute.

5. ADD the sherry, soy sauce, and orange juice to the pan and bring the sauce to a **BOIL** (nickle-sized bubbles will form every few seconds).

6. STIR in the toasted pine nuts, sesame oil, and red pepper flakes. Stir-fry for 1 minute and taste. To adjust seasonings, add more soy sauce if the dish needs to taste saltier, and more sesame oil or sherry to taste sweeter. Serve over rice.

Here's a scrumptious dish for the shrimp lovers in the family.
When served with rice, it's a healthy one-dish meal.

WHAT IS IT? WHERE DO I FIND IT?

FROZEN DEVEINED SHRIMP Deveining shrimp is time-consuming.
Happily, you can buy flash-frozen shrimp that has already been
deveined. Look for it in your supermarket's frozen seafood section.

salmon with lime mustard

Fast and zesty, it's a healthy treat

Serves 6 ✳ *Prep time: 5 minutes* ✳ *Cooking time: 8-10 minutes*

INGREDIENTS

3 tablespoons coarse-grained mustard (see note)

3 tablespoons lime zest (see page 35)

3 tablespoons lime juice

2 teaspoons minced garlic

½ teaspoon salt

¾ teaspoon black pepper

Vegetable oil cooking spray

6 salmon fillets (6 ounces each, with skin on)

1. **PREHEAT** the broiler or grill.

2. **COMBINE** all the ingredients, except the salmon, in a medium-sized bowl.

3. **SPRAY** the broiler pan or grill with vegetable oil cooking spray until it is generously coated. **PLACE** the salmon fillets, skin side down, on the grill or pan.

4. **BRUSH** the top of each fillet with the mustard mixture.

5. **BROIL** or grill the fillets—do not turn them—8 to 10 minutes or until the center of each fillet is still slightly pink.

6. **SERVE** immediately.

WHAT IS IT? WHERE DO I FIND IT?

FRESH SALMON is sold whole or cut into steaks or fillets. Buy the freshest fish you can find in a busy fish market that has a lot of turnover. When making a simple recipe such as this one, cook double the amount of salmon you will need and refrigerate the extra portion. It's wonderful served as a salad over greens in a day or two, or cut into chunks and tossed with hot pasta, dill, and olive oil.

* * *

COARSE-GRAINED MUSTARD is mustard with mustard seeds in it. Smooth mustards have pulverized seeds so you can't see them. Grainy mustards are usually spicier than the smoother Dijon style of mustards.

✳ NOW WHAT? ✳

I don't have any coarse-grained mustard. Can I substitute something else?

Yes, any type of Dijon mustard will work. But the stuff you put on hot dogs won't do.

* * *

I'd like to use salmon steaks instead of fillets. What's the difference?

A salmon steak is horseshoe-shaped, thicker than a fillet, and has skin around its sides. A salmon fillet is much thinner and has no real edge. It will have skin on one side. In this recipe you can substitute a steak for a fillet. They require the same amount of grilling time.

ginger-sesame salmon

Fish with an Asian flair in a foil packet

Serves 6 ✳ *Prep time: 15 minutes* ✳ *Cooking time: 20 minutes*

INGREDIENTS

6 sheets sheets aluminum foil measuring 12 x 18 inches

1 ¼ cups thinly sliced leeks, or 1 large onion, sliced and separated into rings

3 medium carrots, shredded

1 yellow bell pepper, seeded and cut into thin strips

1 red bell pepper, seeded and cut into thin strips

6 salmon fillets (6 ounces each)

1 teaspoon ground ginger or 1 tablespoon grated fresh ginger (see page 39)

1 teaspoon garlic powder

3 tablespoons rice-wine vinegar, or white vinegar

3 tablespoons sherry

3 teaspoons sesame oil

Salt and black pepper to taste

1. **PREHEAT** the oven to 450°F, or preheat a grill to its highest setting.

2. **PLACE** the leeks, carrots, and yellow and red peppers on the foil sheets, dividing the vegetables evenly.

3. **PLACE** one salmon fillet atop each mound of vegetables.

4. In a small bowl, **MIX** the ginger, garlic powder, vinegar, sherry, and sesame oil.

5. **DRIZZLE** the ginger mixture evenly over the tops of the salmon fillets. Season with salt and pepper.

6. **FOLD** the foil over each fillet, bringing the two opposite edges together to make a ridge across the top of the steak. Fold over the ridge twice so that it seals the foil packet. Place the packets on a baking sheet.

7. **BAKE** the packets 20 minutes or grill them 18 minutes on a covered grill.

8. **REMOVE** the packets from the oven or grill when they are done. Carefully open the packets part way, allowing the

steam to escape, and then open them fully. Transfer the fish and vegetables from each of the foil packets onto individual plates. Serve immediately.

✳ NOW WHAT?! ✳

How can I avoid getting my fingers burned when I open a packet?
Burns occur when a packet (or pot, for that matter) in which food is steamed is opened quickly and a large amount of steam rushes out all at once. After cooking the packets, carefully open a small part of the seal, keeping your hands on each side of the opening instead of over it, and your face turned away from it. Wearing kitchen mitts or gloves can help. After some of the steam has escaped from the small opening, gradually open the rest of the seal.

WHAT IS IT? WHERE DO I FIND IT?

RICE-WINE VINEGAR, used in Asian cooking, has a smooth mild flavor. Look for it near the other vinegars in the salad dressing section at your supermarket.

• • •

SESAME OIL, another ingredient that comes from Asia, is made from pressing sesame seeds. It's also available in most supermarkets.

scallop and mushroom sauté

Last-minute cooking, melt-in-your-mouth taste

Serves 6-8 ✳ *Prep time: 15 minutes* ✳ *Cooking time: 8-10 minutes*

INGREDIENTS

- 2 **pounds** bay scallops
- 1 **cup** dry white wine or vermouth
- 2 **tablespoons** lemon juice
- 1 **pound** button or shiitake mushrooms, thinly sliced
- ½ **cup** diced onion
- 2 **tablespoons** butter
- 2 **tablespoons** olive oil
- 1 **teaspoon** dried oregano
- 1 **teaspoon** arrowroot (see note), or 2 teaspoons corn-starch
- 3 **tablespoons** cold water
- 1 **teaspoon** dried parsley
- 2 **tablespoons** grated Parmesan cheese

salt and pepper to taste

1. **PLACE** the scallops, wine, and lemon juice in a large skillet over medium-low heat. **SIMMER** the scallops (pearl-sized bubbles will form in the liquid every few seconds) for 1 to 2 minutes, just until the scallops become opaque. Do not overcook or the scallops will become tough.

2. **DRAIN** the liquid from the skillet into a small bowl and set it aside. Transfer the scallops to another small bowl and set them aside.

3. **RETURN** the skillet to the stove, add the mushrooms, onion, butter, and oil to the skillet. Increase the heat to medium-high and cook for 3 to 5 miutes, stirring occasionally. Add the oregano and stir to combine the mixture thoroughly.

4. **RETURN** the scallops to the pan and stir to combine. Transfer the scallop-mushroom mixture to a warm bowl and set aside.

5. In a small bowl, **MIX** the arrowroot and water together and add the mixture to the same skillet and stir. Add the reserved cooking liquid, parsley, cheese, and seasonings, and stir to combine the mixture thoroughly. Simmer the

mixture for about 2 minutes, stirring constantly, until the sauce is smooth and slightly thickened.

6. ADD the scallop-mushroom mixture to the skillet. Heat for 1 minute, until it is warm. Transfer to a warm platter and serve immediately.

❋ NOW WHAT? ❋

⊙ My scallops are always tough. What am I doing wrong?

You probably are cooking them too long. Barely cooking them gives the freshest-tasting, most tender results.

• • •

⊙ I can only get sea scallops. Can I use them in this recipe?

Yes, but you will need to pat them dry with a paper towel before cooking to remove any excess water, and cook them just a bit longer, up to 3 minutes, depending on their size.

• • •

⊙ What should I serve with this recipe to soak up the pan juices?

It goes well over brown or white rice or over pasta, such as bowties, penne, or fusilli.

WHAT IS IT? WHERE DO I FIND IT?

ARROWROOT, available in supermarkets and natural food stores, is a fine powder used as a thickening agent. It thickens at lower temperatures than flour or cornstarch, and its flavor is much subtler. But it will lump unless mixed with a little cold liquid before adding it to a hot mixture.

rosemary shrimp

A delicacy ready in less than 15 minutes

Serves 4-6 ✳ *Prep time: 5 minutes* ✳ *Cooking time: 6-8 minutes*

INGREDIENTS

5 tablespoons olive oil

½ **cup** minced yellow onion

2 cloves garlic, minced

2 teaspoons dried rosemary, crumbled, or 2 tablespoons minced fresh rosemary

1¾ **pounds** large, frozen, deveined shrimp (see page 159), thawed

⅔ **cup** dry white wine

Salt and black pepper to taste

1. HEAT the oil in a large skillet over high heat.

2. ADD the onion, garlic, and rosemary and **SAUTÉ** (cook over medium-high heat, checking frequently so the food doesn't burn), stirring occasionally, about 2 minutes.

3. ADD the shrimp and continue sautéing until they are heated through, about 2 minutes.

4. ADD the wine and continue sautéing for 1 minute longer, stirring constantly.

5. SEASON the shrimp with salt and pepper to taste. Serve immediately.

WHAT IS IT? WHERE DO I FIND IT?

FRESH ROSEMARY, a highly aromatic herb, is usually used chopped or snipped (cut with scissors) because its needle-like leaves are rather stiff. Look for it among the fresh herbs in the produce section of your supermarket.

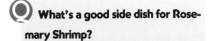

✳ NOW WHAT? ✳

Q **What's a good side dish for Rosemary Shrimp?**

Wild Rice Salad (page 60) is a great complement to the rosemary and shrimp.

grilled tuna with fruit salsa

Summary fruit is the perfect complement to tuna

Serves 4 ✳ *Prep time: 8 minutes* ✳ *Cooking time: 8 minutes*

INGREDIENTS

- ¾ **cup** coarsely chopped honeydew melon
- ¾ **cup** coarsely chopped cantaloupe
- 2 **small** peaches, peeled and chopped
- 1 **cup** chopped red onion
- 2 **tablespoons** dried parsley
- ¼ **cup** chopped fresh cilantro
- 3 **tablespoons** olive oil
- 3 **tablespoons** lime juice
- 4 fresh tuna steaks (6 ounces each), about 1 inch thick

1. **PREPARE** the grill so that the heat is medium-high, or preheat the broiler.

2. **COMBINE** the honeydew, cantaloupe, peaches, onion, parsely, cilantro, 2 tablespoons of the olive oil, and the lime juice in a medium-sized bowl.

3. **BRUSH** the tuna steaks with the remaining olive oil.

4. **GRILL** or broil the tuna about 3 to 4 minutes per side, or until the flesh is still pink in the middle when a slender knife is inserted in the center of a steak.

5. **TRANSFER** the steaks to warm dinner plates and spoon the salsa alongside them. Serve immediately.

✳ NOW WHAT?! ✳

If I use a broiler instead of a grill, do I cook the fish any differently?
Everything is the same, including the cooking time.

• • •

If I can't find a ripe melon in the market, can I substitute something else?
Yes, fruit such as nectarines, papaya, and mango will work well. Or add them to the mixture.

WHAT IS IT? WHERE DO I FIND IT?

MELONS are the pride of produce sections and farmers' stands, especially in the summer when they are at their best. If fully ripe, a melon can be kept in the refrigerator for up to five days. Store underripe melons at room temperature, preferably in a paper bag pierced with several holes, until they ripen. Adding an apple to the bag will speed the process.

Desserts

Indulge yourself with these award-winning desserts (from left to right): Carrot Cake; Quick Cheesecake Tart; Old-Fashioned Lime Pie; and Oatmeal Raisin Cookies.

ginger cookies

Soft, chewy morsels with plenty of spice

Yields: 30 cookies ✳ *Prep time: 20 minutes* ✳ *Chilling time: 1 hour*
✳ *Cooking time: 10-12 minutes*

INGREDIENTS

- **2 cups** all-purpose flour
- **2 ½ teaspoons** ground ginger
- **1 ½ teaspoons** ground cinnamon
- **1 teaspoon** ground cloves
- **¼ teaspoon** ground allspice
- **2 teaspoons** baking soda
- **½ teaspoon** salt
- **¾ cup** crystallized ginger, chopped
- **1 cup plus 2 tablespoons** dark brown sugar, packed
- **½ cup** vegetable shortening, at room temperature
- **¼ cup** sweet (unsalted) butter, softened
- **1 large** egg, lightly beaten
- **¼ cup** light molasses
- Vegetable oil cooking spray
- white sugar for dusting

1. COMBINE the first 7 ingredients in a medium-sized bowl and stir until they are blended.

2. ADD the crystallized ginger to the flour mixture and set the bowl aside.

3. BEAT the brown sugar, shortening, and butter in a large mixing bowl, using an electric mixer, until the mixture is smooth and creamy.

4. ADD the egg and molasses to the sugar mixture and beat until thoroughly blended.

5. ADD the flour mixture to the sugar and egg mixture, a little at a time, stirring to combine them.

6. COVER the bowl and refrigerate the dough for at least 1 hour. (You may refrigerate the dough overnight if you want.)

7. PREHEAT the oven to 350°F. Spray two cookie sheets lightly with cooking spray. Spoon the sugar for dusting onto a small plate and set aside.

8. FORM the cookie dough into 1-inch balls by rolling them in the palm of your hand. When done, roll the balls in sugar until they are coated completely. Place the balls on the cookie sheets about 2 inches apart, to allow the cookies to spread during baking.

9. BAKE the cookies just until cracks appear on their tops, about 10 minutes. The cookies should still be slightly soft. Remove the cookies from the oven, and allow them to cool on the baking sheets for 5 minutes.

10. TRANSFER the cookies to wire racks and allow them to cool completely. Serve or store in a zip-top plastic bag in the freezer.

WHAT IS IT? WHERE DO I FIND IT?

CRYSTALLIZED GINGER Available in most supermarkets, it is made by cooking fresh ginger in sugar syrup and coating it with coarse sugar. The dried powdered ginger is far less potent, and should not be substituted for the crystallized ginger in these cookies.

* * *

MOLASSES Most supermarkets carry this sweetener, made of juice pressed from sugar cane that has been slowly cooked until much of the moisture has evaporated and the syrup is dark and very thick. Light or dark molasses can be used in the cookie recipe; the dark has a more robust flavor.

* * *

VEGETABLE SHORTENING This is a solid fat that gives the ginger cookie its traditional texture. Substituting butter or liquid vegetable oil is not receommended for this recipe.

❋ **NOW WHAT?!** ❋

🔵 **I've seen "blackstrap" molasses in the stores. Is it good in this recipe?**
It's very thick and dark, and somewhat bitter tasting, due to longer cooking when it was made. It will give the cookies a stronger flavor.

• • •

🔵 **Why mix the butter and sugar, then the eggs, then the dry ingredients? Why not just dump in all the ingredients together?**
Butter and sugar tend to lump if egg (a binding agent) is added before they are creamed together. The minute dry ingredients such as baking powder and soda get wet they will start working to release gases that make the cookies rise. Mixing them first with the flour allows them to be added evenly to the wet ingredients, so the cookie batter will rise more evenly.

oatmeal raisin cookies

Chewy and buttery and full of plump raisins

Yields: 36 cookies ✳ *Prep time: 30 minutes* ✳ *Cooking time: 10 minutes*

INGREDIENTS

Vegetable oil cooking spray

- ¾ **cup** sweet (unsalted) butter, at room temperature
- 1 **cup**, plus 2 tablespoons light brown sugar, packed
- ½ **cup** granulated sugar
- 1 egg plus 1 egg white, lightly beaten
- ½ **cup** low-fat milk
- 1½ **teaspoons** vanilla extract
- 1¼ **cup** raisins
- 3 **cups** quick-cooking rolled oats
- 1¼ **cups** all-purpose flour
- ½ **teaspoon** baking soda
- ½ **teaspoon** salt

1. PREHEAT the oven to 350°F. Lightly spray four cookie sheets (also called baking sheets) with cooking spray.

2. BEAT the butter and sugars in a large mixing bowl, using an electric mixer, until the mixture is smooth and creamy. Set the bowl aside.

3. COMBINE the eggs, milk, and vanilla in a small mixing bowl. Add the raisins and stir until the raisins are coated. Set the bowl aside.

4. In a medium-sized bowl, **STIR** together the oats, flour, baking soda, and salt.

5. ADD the raisin mixture to the butter mixture, and stir until they are combined.

6. ADD the flour mixture to the wet mixture, a little at a time, stirring just enough to combine the two mixtures.

7. DROP large teaspoonfuls of the batter onto the cookie sheets, spacing the drops of batter about 2 inches apart, to allow them to spread during baking.

8. BAKE the cookies for about 10 minutes, or until they are golden brown. Remove the cookies from the oven and let them cool on the pans for about 5 minutes.

9. TRANSFER the cookies to wire racks and allow them to cool completely. Serve immediately, or store in a zip-top plastic bag in the freezer for a month.

❋ NOW WHAT? ❋

Some of my cookies are done before the others. Why?
Most ovens have some spots that are hotter than others, so the cookies may not bake evenly. To even up the process, rotate the baking sheets front to back and top to bottom during baking. The shelves should be about six inches apart to ensure proper air circulation.

• • •

What if I like nuts in my oatmeal raisin cookies?
Stir in 1/2 to 1 cup of chopped pecans or walnuts after the flour mixture has been added (Step 6, opposite).

• • •

I've heard cooks talk about "creaming" ingredients. What does that mean?
When butter and sugar are mixed together they take on a creamy texture (Step 2, opposite), and are said to be "creamed" together. The process can be done by hand, but it is laborious; using an electric mixer is the easier way.

WHAT IS IT? WHERE DO I FIND IT?

OATS The rolled variety—steamed, flattened, and cut into flakes—can be found in any supermarket. They're what you use to make oatmeal. Quick-cooking or regular rolled oats are interchangeable in this cookie recipe. But don't use the instant variety, since it has been precooked and will turn into lumps. Also avoid steel-cut oats, also called Scotch- or Irish-style oats. They take far too long to cook to be suitable for this cookie recipe.

Plump oatmeal raisin cookies—a delectable afternoon treat.

apple pie

Granny Smith apple filling and a homemade pie crust—pure comfort food, especially topped with ice cream

Serves 6-8 ✳ *Prep time: 30 minutes* ✳ *Cooking time: 1 hour*

INGREDIENTS

- **3 cups** all-purpose flour
- **1 teaspoon** salt
- **1 cup** cold sweet (unsalted) butter, cut into small pieces
- **6 (or more) tablespoons** ice water
- **3 tablespoons** lemon juice

or

- **1 prepared 9-inch** pie shell with top crust, unbaked

PIE FILLING

- **¼ cup** granulated sugar
- **2 tablespoons** flour
- **¼ teaspoon** ground nutmeg
- **1 teaspoon** ground cinnamon
- **2 tablespoons** lemon juice
- **10** Granny Smith apples, peeled, cored, and thinly sliced (see note)
- **2 tablespoons** sweet (unsalted) butter, cut into small pieces

for the crust

1. COMBINE flour and salt in a medium-sized bowl. **ADD** the butter and mix it into the flour mixture with a fork or your fingers. (Or combine in a food processor fitted with a metal blade.) When the mixture resembles oatmeal, **ADD** water and lemon juice a little at a time, until the dough just holds together. **DIVIDE** the dough in half. Form each half into a ball, wrap each in plastic wrap, and place them in the freezer for 15 minutes.

2. Remove the dough from the freezer. On a lightly floured surface, **ROLL** one dough ball into a circle about 2 inches larger than the pie pan; this is the bottom crust. Roll the other ball into a circle about half an inch larger than the pan; this is the top crust. Work quickly and try to handle the dough as little as possible.

3. ARRANGE the bottom crust in an 8- or 9-inch pie pan. The edge of the crust should overlap the rim of the pan slightly. Place the top crust on a plate. Cover the crusts with waxed paper and put them in the refrigerator while you prepare the pie filling.

for the pie

1. PREHEAT the oven to 400°F.

2. COMBINE the sugar, flour, nutmeg, cinnamon, and lemon juice in a small bowl.

3. PLACE the sliced apples in a large bowl. Add the sugar mixture, and toss until the slices are evenly coated. Take the pie crusts out of the refrigerator and **ARRANGE** the apples in layers in the pan. Scatter the butter pieces over the apples.

4. LAY the top crust over apples. Trim the edge with a knife; discard the excess crust. Seal the crusts together by pressing down all around the edge with a fork or your fingers. Using a sharp knife, poke six ½-inch-long slits in the top crust.

5. BAKE pie until the crust is very lightly browned, about 1 hour. If the edges brown too quickly, lay strips of aluminum foil around the edges, and leave them there for the remainder of the baking time.

6. REMOVE the pie from the oven. Place it on a wire rack and let it cool for 10 minutes. Serve the pie warm with vanilla ice cream.

❋ NOW WHAT?! ❋

Why does the recipe say that the pie dough should not be handled too much?
Overhandling the pie dough tends to make the finished pie crust tough or less flaky. Adding too much liquid can also toughen the crust. As you practice making pie dough by making more pies, you will find you are able to use smaller amounts of liquid, and will gradually handle the dough less and less.

* * *

How do I keep my apples from turning brown after I slice them?
Warm air will turn cut fruit brown. Stop the browning by keeping your just-sliced apples in a bowl of cold water. You can also sprinkle them with lemon juice.

WHAT IS IT? WHERE DO I FIND IT?

GRANNY SMITH APPLES Most produce sections in supermarkets and greengrocers carry these tart, green apples that are perfect for pies. Be careful about substituting other apple varieties for Granny Smiths, unless you know that they are recommended for pies.

chocolate midnight pie

Like a dense fudge brownie in a pie shape— totally decadent!

Serves 8 ✳ *Prep time: 15 minutes* ✳ *Cooking time: 25 minutes*

INGREDIENTS

Vegetable oil cooking spray

- ½ **cup** butter
- 2½ **squares** unsweetened chocolate (2½ ounces)
- 2 **large** eggs, lightly beaten
- 1 **cup** sugar
- ¼ **cup** plus 1 teaspoon flour
- ¼ **teaspoon** salt
- 1 **teaspoon** vanilla

Garnish (optional): fresh raspberries and whipped cream or vanilla ice cream

1. PREHEAT the oven to 350°F. Spray a 9-inch-wide glass pie dish with cooking spray and set it aside.

2. MELT the butter and chocolate in a small saucepan over very low heat, stirring frequently so that the chocolate does not burn. When the mixture is smooth, remove it from the heat and set aside.

3. BEAT the eggs and sugar in a medium-sized bowl, using an electric mixer for about 3 minutes. Add the warm chocolate mixture to the bowl; next add the flour, salt, and vanilla. Mix thoroughly until the mixture is smooth.

4. POUR the mixture into the pie dish.

5. BAKE the pie for 25 minutes. Remove the pie from the oven and allow it to cool slightly. Serve warm or at room temperature garnished with fresh raspberries and whipped cream or vanilla ice cream.

Add whipped cream and fresh raspberries to turn this simple chocolate pie into an elegant, delicious dessert.

WHAT IS IT? WHERE DO I FIND IT?

UNSWEETENED CHOCOLATE is chocolate without any added sugar. It is available in supermarkets. It's ideal for cooking because you can add as much or as little sweetening as your recipe calls for. You might want to experiment with an imported chocolate, available in some specialty food shops, since the flavor of each country's chocolate differs slightly.

✴ NOW WHAT?! ✴

Q Whenever I melt chocolate, it forms clumps. Why?

Although chocolate can be melted with other ingredients, such as butter or a liqueur, a single drop of water will cause it to "seize" (clump and harden). Sometimes you can correct seizing by adding vegetable oil immediately to the chocolate (1 tablespoon of a neutral-tasting oil, such as canola oil, per 6 ounces chocolate), and stirring the mixture slowly over very low heat until it is smooth.

• • •

Q I can't seem to melt chocolate without it taking on a bitter taste. Why?

You melted it over heat that was too high, so that it scorched. Very low heat and constant stirring is needed to melt chocolate slowly and prevent it from burning.

old-fashioned lime pie

A cool summertime dessert

Serves 8 ✳ *Prep time: 30 minutes* ✳ *Cooking time: 30 minutes* ✳ *Chilling time: 3 hours*

INGREDIENTS

- **5 ounces** vanilla wafer cookies
- ½ **stick** sweet (unsalted) butter, melted
- 1 ½ **tablespoons** lime zest (see page 85)
- ¼ **teaspoon** ground cinnamon
- 1 **can (14 ounces)** sweetened condensed milk
- ¾ **cup** lime juice
- 2 **extra-large** eggs, beaten lightly
- **Garnish** (optional): Whipped cream

1. PREHEAT the oven to 350°F.

2. GRIND the vanilla wafers in a blender or the bowl of a food processor fitted with a steel blade. Add the melted butter, 1 teaspoon of the lime zest, and the cinnamon. **PROCESS** the crumb mixture for a few seconds more, until it is thoroughly moist. Transfer the crumb mixture to an ungreased 9-inch glass pie pan and firmly press the mixture onto the bottom and up the sides of the dish.

3. BAKE the crumb crust for about 10 minutes, until golden brown. Remove the crust from oven.

4. PLACE the condensed milk, lime juice, and remaining lime zest in a medium-sized bowl and use a whisk to mix them together. Add the eggs and whisk the filling mixture until it is slightly frothy.

5. POUR the filling into the warm crust. Bake the pie for 20 minutes, or until the filling is set. Cool the pie slightly, about 15 minutes, or until the glass pan is barely warm.

6. REFRIGERATE the pie for at least 3 hours. (The pie can be covered with plastic wrap and refrigerated for several days.)

7. REMOVE the pie from the refrigerator just before serving. Cut into wedges and serve plain or topped with whipped cream.

WHAT IS IT? WHERE DO I FIND IT?

SWEETENED CONDENSED MILK This is canned whole milk that is very thick, since 60 percent of the water in the milk has been removed and sugar has been added. Don't try to substitute regular condensed milk or plain milk; the pie owes its silky texture to this particular milk product. You can find it in the baking section of most supermarkets.

❋ **NOW WHAT?** ❋

Does it matter if you bake a pie in a glass pan or an aluminum one?
Each type of pie dish or pan has its own special use, so it is best to use the one your recipe calls for. Glass pie dishes as well as dark-metal and dull-metal pans all absorb heat and produce a crisp, golden-brown crust. Shiny aluminum pans produce a pale crust. (If you substitute a glass pie dish in a recipe that calls for another type of pie pan, lower the baking temperature by 25°F.)

Lime pie is light and tart. It makes an ideal ending to a barbeque or grilled fish dinner.

chocolate mousse cake

Fabulous, elegant and easy to make. Plan ahead—it must be chilled overnight

Serves 8-10 ✳ *Prep time: 30 minutes* ✳ *Cooking time: none* ✳ *Chilling time: overnight*

INGREDIENTS

- **8 ounces** chocolate wafer cookies
- **10 tablespoons** sweet (unsalted) butter, melted
- **½ teaspoon** ground cinnamon
- **2¾ cups** semisweet chocolate chips
- **2 extra-large** eggs, whole
- **2 cups** whipping cream
- **4 extra-large** eggs, separated

TOPPING

- **1½ cups** whipping cream
- **1½ tablespoons** granulated sugar
- **1¼ teaspoons** vanilla extract
- **Garnish** (optional): Fresh mint leaves or grated chocolate

1. GRIND chocolate wafers in a blender or food processor fitted with a steel blade (or use purchased crumbs). Transfer the crumbs to a small bowl and stir in the melted butter and cinnamon. Press the mixture onto the bottom of a 9-inch springform pan and half-way up the sides. Place the crust in the refrigerator while making the filling.

2. MELT the chocolate chips in a microwave for 1 to 3 minutes or in a small saucepan over very low heat, stirring frequently to prevent scorching. Remove the melted chocolate from the heat and pour it into a large mixing bowl. Allow the chocolate to cool slightly.

3. ADD the whole eggs to the melted chocolate. Using an electric mixer, beat the mixture for about 1 minute. Add the egg yolks and beat several minutes, scraping down sides of bowl to blend the mixture thoroughly.

4. POUR the whipping cream into a separate mixing bowl and beat the cream with an electric mixer until soft peaks form. Set aside.

5. PLACE the egg whites in another large mixing bowl. Thoroughly wash the beaters of the electric mixer and dry them well. Then, using the mixer, beat the egg whites until stiff peaks form.

6. FOLD the whipped cream and egg whites gently into chocolate mixture, using a rubber spatula, until the ingredients are thoroughly combined and the color is uniform.

7. POUR the mousse mixture into the crumb crust and refrigerate overnight.

for the topping

1. WHIP the cream, sugar and vanilla together until it holds soft peaks and the sugar is dissolved.

2. SPREAD the topping evenly over the cake and refrigerate for 1 hour.

3. When you are ready to serve, **LOOSEN** the sides of the cake using a sharp knife. Release the spring and remove the sides of the springform pan and slide the cake, with the bottom of the pan still attached, onto a serving plate.

4. GARNISH the cake with fresh mint leaves and/or grated chocolate.

☀ NOW WHAT? ☀

Q Can other forms of chocolate be substituted for the chips?
You can use semisweet chocolate bars or squares. Do not use baker's squares, they are too bitter.

• • •

Q How do I use a springform pan?
This clever two-part cake pan has a flat bottom and a collar with a spring release clip that forms the sides. When you release the clip, the sides spring away from the edge of the cake. (Before removing the springform sides, run a knife around the edge between the cake and the collar.) The bottom of the pan can be left in place and used instead of a plate for serving.

• • •

Q When I whip egg whites, how do I tell the difference between soft peaks and stiff peaks?
Whipping egg whites fills them with air bubbles and turns them from a liquid to a foamy solid. The longer you beat them, the more solid (stiff) they become. When you pull your beater blades out, the foam will follow, forming a peak. If the tip of the peak folds over, somewhat like a collie's ear, they are soft; if it stays pointing up, they are stiff.

carrot cake

This is very moist and flavorful. It will keep in the refrigerator for up to a week.

Serves 8 to 10 ✳ *Prep time: 40 minutes* ✳ *Cooking time: 50 minutes*

INGREDIENTS

Vegetable oil cooking spray

- **2 cups** all-purpose flour
- **2 teaspoons** baking powder
- **1 ½ teaspoons** baking soda
- **½ teaspoon** salt
- **2 ¼ teaspoons** ground cinnamon
- **1 teaspoon** ground ginger
- **1 ¾ cups** sugar
- **1 ½ cups** canola oil
- **4 large** eggs
- **2 ½ cups** grated carrots
- **½ cup** chopped walnuts
- **1 cup plus 2 tablespoons** crushed pineapple, drained (save the juice for the icing)

CREAM CHEESE ICING

- **1 pound** reduced-fat cream cheese, softened
- **½ cup** butter, softened
- **2 ½ teaspoons** vanilla extract
- **2 ¾ cup** confectioners sugar
- **3 tablespoons** pineapple juice

for the cake

1. PREHEAT the oven to 350°F. Spray two 9-inch round cake pans with cooking spray.

2. PLACE the flour, baking powder, baking soda, salt, cinnamon, and ginger in a large bowl and stir until combined.

3. PLACE the sugar, oil, and eggs in another large mixing bowl. Using an electric mixer, beat them together for about 5 minutes, until the mixture is smooth.

4. STIR in the carrots, walnuts, and pineapple; then stir in the flour mixture.

5. POUR equal amounts of the cake batter into the pans and bake for 45 to 50 minutes, until a wooden toothpick inserted into the center of one of the cake layers comes out clean.

6. REMOVE pans from the oven and place them on a wire rack to cool for 15 minutes. Then remove the cake layers from the pans and put them on the rack to finish cooling.

Luscious cream cheese frosting makes this tantalizing carrot cake a mouth-watering treat.

for the icing

1. PLACE the cream cheese, butter, and vanilla in a large mixing bowl. Using an electric mixer, beat them together for about 2 minutes, until the mixture is smooth and creamy.

2. BEAT the confectioners sugar into the cream cheese mixture, scraping down the sides of the bowl to make sure that it is combined thoroughly.

3. ADD the pineapple juice, 1 tablespoon at a time, to the cream cheese mixture and beat well. If the icing is too runny, add more confectioners sugar. If the icing is too thick, thin it with more pineapple juice.

to assemble the cake

1. PLACE one cake layer upside down on a serving plate and spread some icing on the top of it. Place the other layer, right side up, on the iced lower layer. The two layers should meet perfectly. Spread the remaining icing on the top of the cake and on the sides. Serve.

WHAT IS IT? WHERE DO I FIND IT?

CONFECTIONERS SUGAR Look for it in the baking section of any supermarket. It is sugar ground into a fine powder, with a bit of cornstarch added as a binder. Its fine consistency allows it to soak up liquid quickly, so that icings such as this one can be made almost instantly.

blueberry buckle

Country cousin to traditional cake, this dessert is full of berries, and topped with a cinnamon-sugar crust.

Serves 10 to 12 ✳ *Prep time: 30 minutes* ✳ *Cooking time: 45 minutes*

INGREDIENTS

Vegetable oil cooking spray

- ½ **cup (1 stick) butter**, room temperature
- ¾ **cup** sugar
- 1 **large** egg, lightly beaten
- ½ **cup** low-fat milk
- 2 **cups** all-purpose flour
- 2 **teaspoons** baking powder
- ¼ **teaspoon** salt
- 3 **cups** blueberries
- 1 **teaspoon** lemon zest, optional (see page 85)

TOPPING

- 1 **cup** firmly packed brown sugar
- ⅔ **cup** all-purpose flour
- 1 ½ **teaspoons** ground cinnamon
- ½ **teaspoon** ground nutmeg
- ½ **cup (1 stick)** sweet (unsalted) butter

for the cake

1. PREHEAT the oven to 375°F. Generously coat a 9-inch square or round deep-dish baking pan with cooking spray. (A deep-dish pan has sides that are 2 inches high.)

3. PLACE the butter and sugar in a medium-sized mixing bowl. Using an electric mixer, beat them together for about 3 minutes, until the mixture is smooth and creamy.

3. ADD the egg and milk to the butter mixture and stir until they are well blended.

4. COMBINE the flour, baking powder, and salt in a medium-sized bowl.

4. ADD the flour mixture to the sugar-and-egg mixture a little at a time, stirring until they are just blended together.

5. FOLD the blueberries gently into the batter. Add the zest. Pour the batter into pan and set it aside.

Buckles are best served warm with a dollop of whipped cream.

for the topping

I. PREPARE the topping. Combine all the ingredients in a medium-sized bowl. Mash them together with a fork until the mixture resembles coarse meal or oatmeal. Sprinkle the mixture over the cake batter.

2. BAKE cake for 45 minutes, or until a wooden toothpick inserted into the center of the cake comes out clean. Serve warm.

✳ NOW WHAT?! ✳

Can other berries be substituted, such as blackberries, raspberries, or strawberries?

Blueberries are traditional in this dish because they don't bleed as much as the other berries do, and they hold their shape well. Use small blueberries, sold as wild Maine blueberries, whenever possible; they are much tastier than the large ones.

peach and blackberry crumb pie

A delicious way to use up ripe peaches

Serves 6-8 ✳ *Prep time: 30 minutes* ✳ *Cooking time: 1 hour*

INGREDIENTS

- **1 unbaked 9-inch** pie shell (prepared or homemade, see page 176)
- ¼ **cup** brown sugar, packed
- **1 teaspoon** cinnamon
- ½ **teaspoon** ground ginger
- ¼ **teaspoon** ground nutmeg
- **5 tablespoons** all-purpose flour
- **4 cups** peaches, peeled and sliced
- **3 cups** blackberries or blueberries
- **1 teaspoon** lemon zest (see page 85)
- 1 ½ **tablespoons** lemon juice

CRUMB TOPPING

- ¾ **cup** all-purpose flour
- ½ **cup** quick oats
- ½ **cup** brown sugar, firmly packed
- ⅔ **cup** almonds, chopped
- **6 tablespoons** butter, chilled

1. **PREHEAT** the oven to 375°F.

2. **PREPARE** the pie crust and place it in a 9-inch glass pie pan. If using a purchased pie crust, transfer it to a 9-inch glass pie pan.

3. **PLACE** the brown sugar, cinnamon, ginger, nutmeg, and flour in a large mixing bowl and stir together. Add the peaches, and toss them until they are well coated with the sugar-flour mixture. Gently fold in the blackberries.

4. **SPOON** the fruit mixture into the pie crust and sprinkle the top of the fruit with the lemon zest and lemon juice.

5. **PREPARE** the crumb topping. In a medium-sized bowl, stir together the flour, oats, brown sugar, and almonds. Add the butter and mash it with a fork until the mixture is crumbly. **SPRINKLE** the crumb mixture evenly over the fruit.

6. **BAKE** the pie for 1 hour. Remove the pan to a wire rack and cool slightly for about 15 minutes. Serve warm.

WHAT IS IT? WHERE DO I FIND IT?

BLACKBERRIES are a joy of summer. Choose plump, glossy, deep-colored berries without hulls. (If the hulls are still attached, the berries are immature and will be very tart.) Fresh blackberries can be refrigerated for up to two days.

* * *

PEACHES are another glory of summer. Look for smooth, round, firm fruit, free from blemishes, with a good white or yellow color. Avoid immature peaches; they have a washed-out look and a plastic taste. Fully ripe peaches should be refrigerated for no longer than two days.

* * *

UNBAKED PASTRY SHELLS can be found in the refrigerated food section of any supermarket. You can also find frozen pie crusts in the freezer section, or make crusts with a packaged mix found in the section with baking ingredients.

✳ NOW WHAT?! ✳

What other fruit can I substitute?

Almost any summer fruit is good in a crumb pie such as this. Try blueberries instead of blackberries; try nectarines instead of peaches or a combination of peaches, nectarines, and several berries.

FIRST PERSON DISASTER

Lemon juice saves the day

I love fruit pies and was getting pretty good at making one that called for sliced peaches. I had just finished slicing the peaches when the phone rang. An emergency: my daughter's ride home never showed after soccer practice. An hour later, back in the kitchen with my daughter, I started back on my pie. Too late; the peaches were all brown and soggy. I tossed them and we had ice cream for dessert instead. When I told a friend what happened, she told me that next time I should sprinkle lemon juice on the freshly sliced fruit to keep it from turning brown.

Sarah T., Bismarck, North Dakota

quick cheesecake tart

Any combination of fruit works as a topping

Serves 6-8 ✷ *Prep time: 30 minutes* ✷ *Cooking time: 15 minutes* ✷ *Chilling time: 30 minutes*

INGREDIENTS

- **1** unbaked pie crust, prepared or homemade (see page 176), at room temperature
- **1 teaspoon** flour for dusting
- **1 package (8 ounces)** light cream cheese, softened
- **2 tablespoons** sugar
- **1 teaspoon** lemon zest (see page 85)
- **3 tablespoons** Amaretto (optional, see note)
- **1 teaspoon** almond extract
- **1 ½ teaspoons** vanilla extract
- **½ pint each** blueberries, raspberries, strawberries, and blackberries
- **2-3** firm peaches or nectarines, peeled and sliced

FOR GLAZE

- **2 tablespoons** apricot preserves
- **2 tablespoons** seedless raspberry preserves

1. PREHEAT the oven to 450°F.

2. DUST the pie crust with flour and place it, flour side down, in a 9-inch tart pan with a removable bottom. Form thick sides by folding in the excess pastry instead of trimming it off. Pierce crust with fork.

3. BAKE the crust 12 to 15 minutes, or until it is lightly browned. Do not worry if the crust cracks. Set aside to cool.

4. PLACE the cream cheese, sugar, lemon zest, Amaretto, and almond and vanilla extracts in a large bowl. Using an electric mixer, beat until blended thoroughly.

5. SPREAD the mixture in the cooled crust and refrigerate until it is firm, 45 minutes to 1 hour. (The tart may be prepared up to this point a day in advance. Cover the tart with foil and keep it refrigerated.)

6. If using blueberries, **MOUND** them in the center of the tart. Surround them with a circle of nectarines or peaches. Place raspberries and blackberries around the outside edge. Or skip the peaches and nectarines and just use berries.

7. PREPARE the glaze. In a small saucepan, **MELT** the preserves over low heat, stirring frequently so they don't burn.

8. BRUSH the glaze over the fruit. Refrigerate the tart until ready to serve.

WHAT IS IT? WHERE DO I FIND IT?

LIGHT CREAM CHEESE can be found in the dairy case of most supermarkets. It is more delicate than regular cream cheese, so it blends better with the fruit and berries.

• • •

ALMOND EXTRACT is oil from the nuts, dissolved in alcohol. Intensely flavorful, extracts are used in small amounts to enhance the taste of cakes and cookies. Look for them in the baking or spice section at your market.

• • •

AMARETTO is an almond-flavored liqueur and adds a lovely flavor and scent to dishes. It also makes a nice after-dinner drink, either by itself or with coffee. Amaretto can be purchased at most liquor stores.

The berries make this cheese tart lighter and fruitier than the traditional cheesecake.

glossary

AL DENTE Slightly underdone with a chewy consistency. Italian for "to the tooth." A term usually applied to the cooking of pasta, but also to vegetables that are not fully cooked.

BAKE To cook by free-circulating dry air in an enclosed space, such as an oven. Baking usually refers to cakes, cookies, pies, etc., as opposed to roasting, which refers to meat.

BARBECUE Technically, to cook meat using indirect heat in an enclosed space over natural woods. However, "barbecue" and "grill' have come to be synonymous, meaning to cook food directly over intense heat, usually out-of-doors, using natural woods or charcoal or gas on a grill, in an open pit, or on a spit.

BASTE To pour, brush, or drizzle a liquid over whatever it is you are cooking in order to moisten it and add flavor. A bulb baster is convenient to use.

BEAT To blend or mix ingredients rapidly so that air is incorporated, resulting in a smooth, creamy mixture that has more volume.

BIND To add an agent or ingredient, such as an egg, to a dish to cement or hold the dish together.

BLANCH To plunge food briefly into boiling water in order to tenderize the food or mellow its flavor. Blanching also enhances the color of vegetables.

BLEND To combine ingredients together to a desired consistency.

BOIL To heat water or other liquids to 212°F (at sea level); bubbles will form on the surface.

BONE To remove the bones from meat, poultry, fish, or game. A boning knife is a handy tool for such chores.

BRAISE To cook meat or vegetables in a small amount of liquid in a tightly closed container. This method is ideal for tougher cuts of meat, firm-fleshed fish, and numerous vegetables.

BREAD To dredge or coat food with bread crumbs.

BROIL To cook with intense heat, usually by placing under the broiling heat element in an oven. (In most ovens, the broiling heat element is on the top, the baking heat element on the bottom.) The high heat seals in juices, allowing the outside to brown, but keeping the inside tender.

BROWN To cook briefly in hot fat, allowing a crust (usually brown) to form on all sides and seal in the juices. This method also enriches the flavor of the food.

CHOP To cut up food with a knife into small, uniform pieces or cubes.

CLARIFY To separate the clear, liquid part of a mixture from the solids.

CREAM To mix a softened ingredient, or a combination of ingredients, until well blended and completely soft. Butter and sugar are often creamed together; remember, you can't overdo it.

CRIMP To decorate the edge of a pie crust by pinching the dough with your fingers or a fork. It serves to seal in the filling on a pie with two crusts.

CURDLE What happens when minute solids separate from the liquid in an egg or cream-based mixture due to being heated too quickly.

CUT or CUT-IN A pastry term, meaning to mix shortening or butter with flour or other dry ingredients until the mixture resembles coarse meal. To do this, you can use two knives and cut the shortening or butter directly into the flour, or use your fingers to mix it into the flour.

DASH A very small quantity, a scant ⅛ teaspoon.

DEGLAZE To create a sauce with the little bits of meat or poultry left over in a pan after browning, sautéing, broiling, or roasting by adding a small amount of liquid, mixing it all up, and allowing it to boil up together.

DEGREASE To remove a layer of fat from the top of a soup, sauce, or stock.

DEVEIN To remove the dark vein that runs along the back of a shrimp using a sharp knife or special deveining tool.

DICE To cut food into equal-sized small cubes, usually ranging in size from 1/8 to 1/4 inch.

DOLLOP A very small amount, usually a teaspoonful.

DRAIN To remove liquid or fat from food, often by placing it a colander or strainer or by placing it on a paper towel.

DREDGE To lightly coat food, usually with flour, cornmeal, or bread crumbs. One quick way to coat food is to put the coating material in a ziptop bag, add the food to be coated, then seal the bag and shake.

DRIZZLE To slowly spatter drops of a liquid over a food in a thin stream.

DUST To sprinkle very lightly with flour or sugar.

FLAKE To test the flesh of a fish to see if it is done by breaking away a small piece or flake with a fork.

FOLD To gently incorporate one ingredient into another not by stirring or beating but by lifting from underneath with a rubber spatula.

FRY To cook food in hot fat in a skillet until brown and crisp.

GARNISH To decorate foods with fresh herbs, edible flowers, fresh vegetables, nuts, or fruit to enhance the appearance of the dish.

GRATE To rub a food against a raspy surface (such as the side of a grater) to get fine shreds or tiny chunks of the food. Used for cheeses and vegetables.

GREASE To lightly coat a pan with a bit of butter, oil, or vegetable oil cooking spray to prevent cooked food from sticking.

GRILL To cook food directly over intense heat on a rack over hot coals, natural wood, or gas. See BARBECUE.

GRIND To turn a solid piece of food into fine pieces or a powder by using a mortar and pestle, a food processor, or a meat grinder.

JULIENNE To cut fresh vegetables or other foods into thin matchstick-size pieces of the same length.

KNEAD To work a finished dough until it is smooth and elastic. Use the palms of your hands on a lightly floured wooden or marbled bread board.

MARINATE To enhance the flavor and tenderize the texture of a food by placing it in a seasoned liquid, usually a combination of oil and spices and some type of acidic liquid, such as vinegar, juice, or wine.

MELT To dissolve a solid or semisolid over slow heat. The term is most commonly associated with butter and chocolate.

MINCE To cut a food into very fine pieces, not larger than 1/8 inch square.

MIX To blend ingredients using a spoon or a fork.

PARBOIL To partially cook food in boiling water or broth. Similar to blanching except the food is left in for a longer period of time when parboiling.

POACH To cook food in a simmering liquid that does not boil. Poaching brings out the full delicate flavor of the food.

POUND To flatten meat or poultry, often between sheets of waxed paper, using a heavy mallet or frying pan. Pounding helps tenderize meat and poultry.

PREHEAT To set an oven or broiler to a certain temperature ten to fifteen minutes before putting food in it.

PRICK To pierce food with the tines of a fork to prevent it from bursting or rising during baking.

PUREE To use a blender or food processor to turn cooked food into a smooth liquid, which is also called a puree.

RECONSTITUTE To rehydrate dry food by soaking it in liquid.

REDUCE To boil a sauce to reduce its volume and intensify its flavor.

REFRESH To stop a food from cooking by running it under cold water or plunging it into cold water.

RENDER To liquify or leach out the solid fat by heating. Usually used when cooking meat or poultry.

ROAST To cook food, usually uncovered, in an enclosed space by the free circulation of dry heat.

SAUTÉ To cook food quickly in a small amount of butter or fat over medium to high heat while turning the food frequently so it doesn't burn.

SCALD To heat a liquid (often milk or cream) over low heat until just below its boiling point.

SHRED To cut or tear a food into thin strips.

SIFT To pass dry ingredients through a fine mesh strainer to remove lumps and lighten the texture (often flour).

SIMMER To cook food, usually a soup or stew, over low heat so that it almost, but never quite reaches a boil. Small bubbles will appear on the surface.

SLIVER To cut a food into extra-thin strips.

SNIP To cut herbs into small bits using scissors or kitchen shears.

STEAM To cook food in a covered container using a small amount of boiling liquid.

STEW To cook food slowly over relatively low heat.

STIR To mix or blend a mixture together in a circular motion using a spoon or other implement, or, if over heat, moving food about to prevent it from burning or curdling.

STIR FRY A cooking method developed by the Chinese which consists of quickly moving food around in a small amount of oil, in a wok or frying pan. The food is lightly coated with the oil, while being constantly stirred in the pan. It is essential that your ingredients be cut, sliced or otherwise prepared and ready at hand for cooking in their proper order without any delays.

STRAIN To remove solids from liquids by pouring through a sieve, strainer or colander.

STUFF To fill a cavity with a mixture; for example poultry, fish, meat, vegetables.

TOAST To brown food by baking it directly under heat.

TOSS To gently mix food using a large spoon or fork to lift it from the bottom.

TRUSS To tie the legs and wings of poultry close to the body using string before roasting in order to preserve it in a compact form and prevent the stuffing from falling out of the cavity.

WHIP To beat a food rapidly, such as cream, either by hand using a fork or whisk or with an electric mixer or food processor. Whipping adds a great deal of air, thereby increasing the volume.

WHISK To mix sauces, dressings, eggs and other liquids using a swift, circular motion, usually with a balloon-shaped wire instrument, also called a whisk.

ZEST The finely grated skin of a citrus fruit (such as lemon, lime or orange.) When making zest be careful not to include the bitter white pith just underneath the surface of the skin. You can use a grater, vegetable peeler, or zester (a special tool used just to make zest) to accomplish this feat.

index

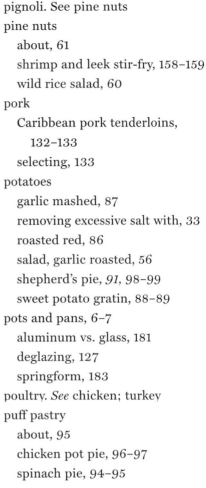

THE AUTHOR: UP CLOSE

Pamela Richards has worked as a professional chef, cookbook collaborator and caterer. But it was as a cooking teacher to beginners that Pam found her true calling. "The trick is to explain the rules of cooking without dampening the fun of it." Who better to write **I'm in the Kitchen, Now What?**! As she tells her students at the beginning of each semester: "Relax, if you can read, you can make anything." Pam lives in Allendale, New Jersey with her two daughters.

PICTURE CREDITS

Sally Mara Sturman 5 (top), **6-11, 51**, back cover;
Robert Milazzo all prepared food photography
PhotoDisc , all other food photography

Editor, Barb Chintz
Leonard Vigliarolo Cover design